KU-257-070

I. M. MARSH COLLEGE

Acc. No. ᴌᴗ , 8 6

Class No. ᴈᴈᴇ
372.9073GOᴌ

M M 372.9073 GOL 1972

LIBRARY
I.M.MARSH COLLEGE OF PHYSICAL EDUCATION
BARKHILL ROAD, LIVERPOOL, 17.

WITHDRAWN

LIVERPOOL POLYTECHNIC LIBRARY

3 1111 00033 9000

GOLDSTROM, J.M
EDUCATION: ELEMENTARY EDUCATION 1780-190
M M 372.9073 GOL 1972

Education
Elementary Education 1780-1900

DAVID & CHARLES SOURCES FOR SOCIAL & ECONOMIC HISTORY

GENERAL EDITOR: *E. R. R. Green*
Director of the Institute of Irish Studies
The Queen's University of Belfast

FREE TRADE
Norman McCord
Reader in Modern History
University of Newcastle upon Tyne

THE FACTORY SYSTEM   VOLUME I BIRTH AND GROWTH
VOLUME II THE FACTORY SYSTEM
AND SOCIETY
J. T. Ward
Senior Lecturer in Economic History
University of Strathclyde

THE ENGLISH POOR LAW 1780–1930
Michael E. Rose
Lecturer in History, University of Manchester

READINGS IN THE DEVELOPMENT OF ECONOMIC ANALYSIS
R. D. Collison Black
Professor of Economics
The Queen's University of Belfast

---

in preparation
NINETEENTH-CENTURY CRIME
John J. Tobias
Senior Tutor of the Special Course
The Police College
Bramshill House
Basingstoke

DAVID & CHARLES SOURCES FOR SOCIAL & ECONOMIC HISTORY

J. M. GOLDSTROM

Lecturer in Economic and Social History
The Queen's University of Belfast

Education

Elementary Education
1780–1900

LIBRARY
I.M. MARSH COLLEGE OF PHYSICAL EDUCATION
BARKHILL ROAD, LIVERPOOL, 17.

DAVID & CHARLES : NEWTON ABBOT

ISBN 0 7153 5475 2

COPYRIGHT NOTICE

© J. M. Goldstrom 1972

All rights reserved. No part of this publication may be reproduced, stored in a retrieval system, or transmitted, in any form or by any means, electronic, mechanical, photocopying, recording or otherwise, without the prior permission of David & Charles (Publishers) Limited.

Set in Baskerville 11 pt 2 pt leaded
and printed in Great Britain
by Latimer Trend & Company Limited Plymouth
for David & Charles (Publishers) Limited
South Devon House   Newton Abbot   Devon

Contents

5

Introduction

Between 1780 and 1900 the population of Great Britain increased fourfold. To feed, house and employ the swelling numbers was beyond the capacity of the old social and economic order and in the period under discussion there were drastic changes in social organisation, production methods and the geographical distribution of the population. Such vast transformations created tensions that were complex and alarming. At the time of the Napoleonic wars and again in the 1830s there was widespread fear of revolution. Malthus was predicting famine if the population increase was not stemmed. Revolution and famine did not come about, but political unrest, class strife and crimes of violence were serious problems, diminishing only as the social structure adapted itself to the needs of an industrialising nation.

Educationists through the period considered that education represented a potential stabilising influence over the working classes. The advocates of mass education in the late eighteenth century had reasoned that the answer to the problems of irreligion and crime and the way to avert revolution lay in the provision of suitable Sunday school education. The Sunday schools certainly taught people to read. But the irreligion, the politically subversive ideas and the crime rate had not been significantly influenced, and in the early nineteenth century energies were directed into the establishment of day schools for poor children. This meant, of course, that children were subjected to school influences for more continuous periods. But still, the problems the Sunday school movement was so confident of eliminating remained. The biblical style of education, universal in these early years of working class education, was weighed and found wanting. By the middle of the century the Bible's importance in the school curriculum had been much diminished and the political economy textbook was taking its place. Thereafter the schools were to adopt an increasingly secular curriculum and concern themselves with fitting the child for his role in an industrial society.

The documents reproduced here illustrate how, slowly and painfully, educational problems were acknowledged and worked out. There were the fundamental questions of who should shoulder the responsibility of education—voluntary church groups or the government? And who should pay for the ever-rising cost of educating poor children who, apart from increasing in numbers, tended to stay longer and longer at school? Should it be the church bodies, or the parents, or the government? There was constant controversy about the best and cheapest methods of teaching, about teacher training, about textbooks, the school syllabus, and the question of a state-supervised school inspectorate.

While we may laugh at the crudities of the assembly-line monitorial systems, and the pretentious nonsense of the Gradgrind educational philosophies, examples of which are to be found among these documents, we must see them in the context of a total transformation of education over the century. At its beginning, practically all working-class children roamed the streets. By its close there was compulsory education of good quality for every working-class child in the land.

PART ONE

Public Concern

Formal education for working-class children existed before 1780, but for very few. The fortunate ones generally attended the charity schools that had been founded by the Society for Promoting Christian Knowledge. Their education was confined to moral and religious instruction, and its purpose was to train them to accept their lowly position in life (Document 1). They learned from specially prepared readers, of stern moral tone, and from the Bible and selections of sermons (2).

It was during the 1780s that serious public interest in working-class education became manifest, and the interest stemmed from various Evangelical groups, both within and outside the Church of England. The Evangelicals were alarmed by working-class lack of interest in religion and the high crime rate, and Robert Raikes and his followers considered that this undesirable state of affairs could be remedied by a widespread establishing of Sunday schools. As these increased in number the Sunday school promoters began to claim that their schools were succeeding in reducing the crime rate and improving church attendance (3). These claims were far from universally accepted and critics of the Sunday school movement in fact argued that any kind of education for the labouring classes was dangerous (4). Sunday schools flourished despite such criticisms, and in the 1790s the teaching material was expanded to include attractively written anthologies of stories, songs and poetry (5).

By the turn of the century Parliament found itself spending more time discussing education, and in 1802 what amounted to an education act for pauper apprentices was passed (6). But there was sharp division of public opinion on education for the poor, and while Parliament deliberated (7) two groups dedicated to the principle of education for working-class children aligned themselves with the day-school systems devised by Joseph Lancaster and his rival, Andrew Bell. Both groups wanted educational provisions to extend to *all* poor children and were well aware that this could be achieved only if costs per head were kept to a minimum (8). Unfortunately for educational progress, early attempts at public debate on the merits of Bell's and Lancaster's schemes degenerated immediately into bitter sectarian wrangling (9).

1 Society for Promoting Christian Knowledge Instructions to Parents

In the early eighteenth century an Anglican organisation, the Society for Promoting Christian Knowledge, began to establish charity schools for giving full-time education to children of the deserving poor. The religious instruction in the schools was designed to condition the children for their humble position in life as servants and labourers. There were virtually no other educational opportunities for poor children in the eighteenth century.

ORDERS
TO BE READ AND GIVEN TO THE PARENTS,
ON THE
ADMITTANCE OF THEIR CHILDREN
INTO THE CHARITY-SCHOOLS;
AND TO BE SET UP IN THEIR HOUSES

1. THAT the parents take care to send their children to school at the school hours, and keep them at home on no pretence whatsoever, except in case of sickness.

2. That they send their children clean washed and combed.

3. That in regard the trustees of this school will take due care that the children shall suffer no injuries by their master or

mistress's correction, which is only designed for their good: the parents shall freely submit their children to undergo the discipline of the school, when guilty of any faults, and forbear coming thither on such occasions: so that the children may not be countenanced in their faults, nor the master or mistress discouraged in the performance of their duty.

4. That it is the duty of parents to keep their children in good order when they are at home, by good example and admonition.

5. That they teach their children at home their catechism, and read the Holy Scriptures, especially on the Lord's Day, and use prayers morning and evening in their families; so that both parents and children may be better informed of their duty, and by a constant and sincere practice thereof procure the blessing of God upon them.

6. That the children attend at the parish Church on the Lord's Day (commonly called *Sunday*), both in the morning and afternoon, and holidays, *Wednesdays* and *Fridays*; and that the master and mistress respectively take notice of their behaviour, and of those who shall be absent at any of those times.

7. That the parents do not take their children out of the school, without first obtaining leave of the trustees; and whatever child shall be so removed without leave, before that time, shall not have clothes and books, nor any other child of these parents taken into the school.

8. If the parents do not observe the said orders, their children are to be dismissed the school, and to forfeit their school clothes.

Ye fathers provoke not your children to wrath, but bring them up in the nurture and admonition of the Lord: having them in subjection with all gravity. Eph. vi. 4. 1 Tim. iii. 4.

Honour thy father and thy mother, that it may be well with thee, and thou mayest live long on the earth. Eph. vi. 2, 3.

Eighteenth-century leaflet still in print in 1827. Bound with *Religious Tracts Dispersed by the Society for Promoting Christian Knowledge, Vol IX, Christian Education and Schools* (1827)

2 The Child's First Book (1780)

Reading matter used in charity schools was the Bible, catechisms, sermons and school readers of stern moral tone. This extract comes from a book published by the Society for Promoting Christian Knowledge and intended for charity schools.

Cau-ti-ons and Di-rec-ti-ons a-gainst the Vi-ces
to which Child-ren are most li-a-ble

My good Child,

THE vi-ces which child-ren of your age are most u-su-al-ly tempt-ed to com-mit, are ly-ing, tak-ing God's name in vain, and steal-ing.

Ly-ing, and pro-fan-ing God's name, are faults which ap-pear ve-ry early: these are found in child-ren al-most as soon as they can speak, and are chief-ly ow-ing to the bad ex-am-ple of their pa-rents, or o-thers of their own fa-mi-ly.

Con-si-der, then, my good child, that no-thing is hid from God; but all things are nak-ed and o-pen to him; that how-e-ver you may be a-ble, by tell-ing a lie, to de-ceive man, you can-not de-ceive God, who search-eth the ve-ry heart and reins; he knows, and will as-sur-ed-ly call you to ac-count for e-ve-ry false word you speak: con-si-der what a vile crea-ture a li-ar is in the eyes of e-ve-ry body; what shame at-tends the crime; and what mis-chief and con-fu-si-on it oc-ca-si-ons in the world: Ob-serve how sel-dom God per-mits this sin to be suc-cess-ful, how fre-quent-ly the li-ar's cou-rage fails him, his own coun-te-nance be-trays him, or his com-pa-ni-ons re-veal his crime.

Re-solve then, my good child, to speak the truth, to ab-hor false-hood, and to suf-fer a-ny thing ra-ther than be tempt-ed to a sin so hate-ful in the sight of God and man, and which will bring great shame and dis-grace to your-self.

Dare to be true, no-thing can need a lie,

The fault that wants it most, grows two there-by.

Be-ware too of get-ting an ha-bit of tak-ing God's ho-ly name in vain, or u-sing a-ny words re-sem-bling oaths; for God is ve-ry jea-lous of his ho-nour. "He will not hold them guilt-less," that is, He will se-vere-ly pu-nish those who pro-fane his name, ei-ther by rash oaths or curs-es, or any o-ther ir-re-ve-rent use of it. Be sure you ne-ver speak of God, nor make men-ti-on of a-ny of his sa-cred ti-tles or names but with the ut-most awe and re-ve-rence. It is a sad thing to think of be-ing ac-count-a-ble here-af-ter for a vast num-ber of these sins which some peo-ple com-mit through mere ha-bit and wretch-ed cus-tom, with-out a-ny temp-ta-ti-on to them, or pos-si-ble plea-sure or pro-fit from them.

There is a third vice which is com-mon in child-ren, and that is pil-fer-ing and steal-ing; which though it may at first con-sist in small things, is ve-ry apt to grow up with them. Take care, there-fore, my good child, that you are not led in-to this sin by the small-ness of the thing which you steal, for it is still what God hath for-bid-den, and what you have no right to: and if you should, through the wick-ed-ness of your own heart, pro-ceed to an ha-bit of it, be-lieve me you are as sure-ly ru-in-ed in this world as you will be con-demn-ed in the next: for what-e-ver be your trade or bu-si-ness, your suc-cess in it will en-tire-ly de-pend up-on your cha-rac-ter of be-ing a just and ho-nest man. *The Child's First Book* part 1 (1820 ed), 14–15

3 Robert Raikes On Sunday Schools

Robert Raikes (1735–1811), proprietor of the *Gloucester Journal*, was the leading publicist of the Sunday School move-ment (though not, as is frequently assumed, its founder), and his articles and letters on the movement drew national atten-tion. In November 1783 he wrote a letter to a Sheffield in-quirer describing his activities in Gloucester. The letter was forwarded to Mr Urban, editor of the *Gentleman's Magazine*.

MR. URBAN, *Sheffield, May 18* [*1784*]
THE Gentleman's Magazine has long been considered as the Repository of every useful and valuable project; I flatter myself, therefore, that you will think the following copy of a letter from

Mr. Raikes of Gloucester, on his new and excellent scheme of Sunday-schools, worth preserving. The importance of the subject, and the benevolent manner in which it is expressed, justly entitle it to the attentive regard of every virtuous man. It is one very direct means to bring about that reformation of manners, which is so much wanted at present, consequently is worthy the especial notice of our clergy and magistrates. I have the pleasure to add, that, by a paragraph in the York Chronicle of the 6th inst. it appears, that the inhabitants of Leeds have, very much to their honour, adopted the plan, and have already eighteen hundred children engaged.—The towns of Huddersfield and Dewsbury are likewise endeavouring to follow so meritorious an example. Yours, etc. etc.

A FRIEND TO VIRTUE.

SIR,   *Gloucester, Nov. 25 [1783]*
    My friend, the mayor, has just communicated to me the letter which you have honoured him with, enquiring into the nature of the Sunday-schools. The beginning of this scheme was entirely owing to accident. Some business leading me one morning into the suburbs of the city, where the lowest of the people (who are principally employed in the pin-manufactory) chiefly reside, I was struck with concern at seeing a groupe of children, wretchedly ragged, at play in the street. I asked an inhabitant whether those children belonged to that part of the town, and lamented their misery and idleness.—Ah! Sir, said the woman to whom I was speaking, could you take a view of this part of the town on a Sunday, you would be shocked indeed; for then the street is filled with multitudes of these wretches, who, released on that day from employment, spend their time in noise and riot, playing at chuck, and cursing and swearing in a manner so horrid, as to convey to any serious mind an idea of hell, rather than any other place. We have a worthy clergyman; said she, curate of our parish, who has put some of them to school; but upon the sabbath, they are all given up to follow their inclinations without restraint, as their parents, totally

abandoned themselvs, have no idea of instilling into the minds of their children principles, to which they themselves are entire strangers.

This conversation suggested to me, that it would be at least a harmless attempt, if it were productive of no good, should some little plan be formed to check this deplorable profanation of the sabbath. I then enquired of the woman, if there were any decent, well-disposed women in the neighbourhood, who kept schools for teaching to read. I presently was directed to four: to these I applied, and made an agreement with them, to receive as many children as I should send upon the Sunday, whom they were to instruct in reading, and in the church catechism.—For this I engaged to pay them each a shilling for their day's employment. The women seemed pleased with the proposal. I then waited on the clergyman before-mentioned, and imparted to him my plan; he was so much satisfied with the idea, that he engaged to lend his assistance, by going round to the schools on a Sunday afternoon, to examine the progress that was made, and to enforce order and decorum among such a set of little heathens.

This, Sir, was the commencement of the plan. It is now about three years since we began, and I could wish you were here to make enquiry into the effect.—A woman who lives in a lane where I had fixed a school, told me some time ago, that the place was quite a heaven upon Sundays, compared to what it used to be. The numbers who have learned to read and say their catechism are so great that I am astonished at it. Upon the Sunday afternoon, the mistresses take their scholars to church, a place into which neither they nor their ancestors had ever before entered, with a view to the glory of God. But what is yet more extraordinary, within this month, these little raggamuffins have in great numbers taken it into their heads to frequent the early morning prayers, which are held every morning at the cathedral at seven o'clock. I believe there were near fifty this morning. They assemble at the house of one of the mistresses, and walk before her to church, two and two, in as much order as a company of soldiers. I am generally at church, and after

B

service they all come round me to make their bow; and, if any animosities have arisen, to make complaints. The great principle I inculcate, is, to be kind and good-natured to each other; not to provoke one another; to be dutiful to their parents; not to offend God by cursing and swearing, and such little plain precepts as all may comprehend. As my profession is that of a printer, I have printed a little book, which I gave amongst them; and some friends of mine, subscribers to the Society for promoting Christian knowledge, sometimes make me a present of a parcel of Bibles, Testaments, etc. which I distribute as rewards to the deserving. The success that has attended this scheme has induced one or two of my friends to adopt the plan, and set up Sunday schools in other parts of the city, and now a whole parish has taken up the object; so that I flatter myself in time the good effects will appear so conspicuous as to become generally adopted. The number of children at present thus engaged on the sabbath are between two and three hundred, and they are increasing every week, as the benefit is universally seen. I have endeavoured to engage the clergy of my acquaintance that reside in their parishes; one has entered into the scheme with great fervour, and it was in order to excite others to follow the example, that I inserted in my paper the paragraph which I suppose you saw copied into the London papers. I cannot express to you the pleasure I often receive in discovering genius, and innate good dispositions, among this little multitude. It is botanising in human nature. I have often, too, the satisfaction of receiving thanks from parents, for the reformation they perceive in their children. Often I have given them kind admonitions, which I always do in the mildest and gentlest manner. The going among them, doing them little kindnesses, distributing trifling rewards, and ingratiating myself with them, I hear, have given me an ascendency, greater than I ever could have imagined; for I am told by their mistresses that they are very much afraid of my displeasure. If you ever pass thro' Gloucester, I shall be happy to pay my respects to you, and to shew you the effects of this effort at civilization. If the glory of

God be promoted in any, even the smallest degree, society must reap some benefit. If good seed be sown in the mind at an early period of human life, though it shews itself not again for many years, it may please God, at some future period, to cause it to spring up, and to bring forth a plentiful harvest. With regard to the rules adopted, I only require that they come to the school on Sunday as clean as possible. Many were at first deterred because they wanted decent clothing, but I could not undertake to supply this defect. I argue, therefore, if you can loiter about without shoes, and in a ragged coat, you may as well come to school, and learn what may tend to your good in that garb. I reject none on that footing. All that I require, are clean hands, clean face, and the hair combed; if you have no clean shirt, come in that which you have on. The want of decent apparel at first kept great numbers at a distance, but they now begin to grow wiser, and all are pressing to learn. I have had the good luck to procure places for some that were deserving, which has been of great use. You will understand that these children are from 6 years old to 12 or 14. Boys and girls above this age, who have been totally undisciplined, are generally too refractory for this government. A reformation in society seems to me only practicable by establishing notices of duty, and practical habits of order and decorum, at an early stage—but whither am I running? I am ashamed to see how much I have trespassed on your patience; but I thought the most complete idea of Sunday-schools, was to be conveyed to you by telling what first suggested the thought—the same sentiments would have arisen in your mind, had they happened to have been called forth as they were suggested to me.

I have no doubt that you will find great improvement to be made on this plan. The minds of men have taken great hold on that prejudice, that we are to do nothing on the sabbath day, which may be deemed labour, and therefore we are to be excused from all application of mind as well as body. The rooting out this prejudice is the point I aim at as my favourite object. Our Saviour takes particular pains to manifest, that whatever tended to promote the health and happiness of our fellow creatures, were sacrifices peculiarly acceptable on that day. I do not think I have written so long a letter for some years. But you will excuse me—my heart is warm in the cause. I think this is the kind of reformation most requisite in this kingdom. Let our patriots employ themselves in rescuing their countrymen from that despotism, which tyrannical passions and vicious inclinations exercise over them, and they will find that true liberty and national welfare are more essentially promoted, than by any reform in Parliament.

As often as I have attempted to conclude, some new idea has arisen. This is strange, as I am writing to a person whom I never have, and perhaps never may see—but I have felt that we think alike. I shall therefore only add my ardent wishes, that your views of promoting the happiness of society may be attended with every possible success, conscious that your own internal enjoyment will thereby be considerably advanced. I have the honour to be, Sir,

Yours, etc.   R. RAIKES.

₊ It is with pleasure we give place to this benevolent plan; which promises fair to transmit the name of Mr. Raikes to later posterity. *Gentleman's Magazine* (June 1784), 410–12

---

4 Gentleman's Magazine A Little Learning is a Dangerous Thing

An anonymous correspondent in the *Gentleman's Magazine* is sceptical of the value of Sunday schools.

MR. URBAN,   *Sept. 24 [1797]*
The late establishment of Sunday-schools, though it has been applauded by many people as a benevolent and useful institution, is, in my opinion, far from deserving that character. It is, indeed, calculated to give the children of the poor a small tincture of learning; but, it has been rightly observed, that

"A little learning is a dangerous thing."

The advocates for this institution pretend, with an air of great plausibility, that it is highly expedient that the children of the poor should be taught to read the Scriptures, and learn their duty to God. If this were the only consequence attending the institution of Sunday-schools, they would be liable to no objection; but this is far from being the case. The idleness of six days infinitely counterbalances the instructions of the seventh; for, it can be of little advantage to repeat the Ten Commandments on the Sunday, and violate every moral duty all the rest of the week. The habitual practice of lying, swearing, stealing, fighting, and other low and sordid vices, will totally obliterate all the good advice they can derive from a hasty and imperfect repetition of their Catechism; and it would be infinitely more advantageous to the community in general to train these children in habits of useful industry for six days in the week, than to teach them the mere theoretical principles of morality; which, in the present instance, will have no more effect on their lives and conversation than so many definitions in mathematicks.

The practice of mankind, we must confess, is more effectually controlled by the laws of society than the sanctions of a future state; and I am sorry to say, that the fear of the gallows operates more strongly on the multitude than the fear of God; merely because the one presents an immediate punishment, the other a retribution out of sight and remote.

You will say, that it must be a considerable advantage to restrain the youth, who are born in indigent circumstances, destitute of either good example or good instruction, from violating the Christian Sabbath by their usual irregularities; and that it is a very material acquisition to keep that day with some degree of veneration.

This may be true; but, let it be remembered that, in a rational and philosophical view, the morality of one day can be no compensation for the immorality of six; and that, to make the scheme effectual, it is absolutely necessary to combine a proper discipline, and a habit of industry, with the instruction of the Sunday; otherwise the establishment is perfectly useless.

Industry is the great principle of duty that ought to be inculcated on the lowest class of the people, as it is the best and most effectual barrier against vices of every kind; as it occupies the mind, and leaves no vacancy for licentious thoughts and mischievous projects. A young ruffian, brought up from his infancy in every sordid vice, will not be restrained by the repetition of his Catechism for half an hour in the week, if he is let loose to follow his own inclinations for six days afterwards. He will make this weekly task a pretence with his parents for consummate idleness every other day; for, it has been known, that a boy in this situation has absolutely refused to obey his parents, or perform the least service at home, by pleading that he has had a lesson to learn, or a few verses to repeat on his return to school.

It will, I think, be found upon examination, that a small tincture of what is usually called learning generally infuses a spirit of ambition, and prompts a man to raise himself from a life of drudgery to a state of more ease and emolument. If he is disappointed in his views, and his ambition exceeds his income, he has recourse to fraud and other criminal pursuits to gratify his desires; and an ignominious execution is commonly the necessary consequence. There are, perhaps, more criminals among that class of men who have had a superficial education than among those who have never been taught either to write or read. The laborious occupations of life must be performed by those who have been born in the lowest stations; but no one will be willing to undertake the most servile employment, or the meanest drudgery, if his mind is opened, and his abilities increased, by any tolerable share of scholastic improvement: yet these employments and this drudgery must be necessarily performed. Society cannot possibly subsist without them; and, surely, none can be more properly fitted for this purpose than those who have been born in a state of poverty. The man, whose mind is not illuminated by one ray of science, can discharge his duty in the most sordid employment without the smallest views of raising himself to a higher station, and can take his rest at night in perfect satisfaction and content. His ignorance is a balm that soothes his mind into stupidity and repose, and excludes every emotion of discontent, pride, and ambition. A man of no literature will seldom attempt to form insurrections, or plan an idle scheme for the reformation of the State. Conscious of his inability, he will withdraw from such associations; while those who are qualified by a tincture of superficial learning, and have imbibed the pernicious doctrines of seditious writers, will be the first to excite rebellions, and convert a flourishing kingdom into a state of anarchy and confusion. We have lately seen what dangers have been occasioned by idle scribblers, alehouse politicians, and seditious declamers; and it would have been happy for the community if those *active citizens*, those turbulent members of society, had never extended their ideas beyond the *hammer*, the *shovel*, or the *last*.

We may therefore conclude, that the Sunday-school is so far from being a wise, useful, or prudential institution, that it is in reality productive of no valuable advantage; but, on the contrary, subversive of that order, that industry, that peace and tranquillity which constitute the happiness of society; and that, so far from deserving encouragement and applause, it merits our contempt, and ought to be exploded as the vain and chimerical invention of a visionary projector.

EUSEBIUS
Gentleman's Magazine, (Oct 1797), 819–20

5 Hannah More   The Two Weavers

Hannah More (1745–1833) wrote many stories and poems for Sunday schools. This one demonstrates that it is best for poor people to be content in the station of life that God has allotted to them.

TURN THE CARPET;
OR, THE
TWO WEAVERS:
A NEW SONG

I

As at their work two Weavers sat,
Beguiling time with friendly chat;
They touch'd upon the price of meat,
So high, a Weaver scarce could eat.

II

What with my brats and sickly wife,
Quoth Dick, I'm almost tir'd of life;
So hard my work, so poor my fare,
'Tis more than mortal man can bear.

III

How glorious is the rich man's state!
His house so fine! his wealth so great.
Heaven is unjust you must agree,
Why all to him, why none to me?

IV

In spite of what the Scripture teaches,
In spite of all the Parson preaches,
This world (indeed I've thought so long)
Is rul'd, methinks, extremely wrong.

V

Wheree'er I look, howe'er I range,
'Tis all confus'd, and hard, and strange;
The good are troubled and oppress'd,
And all the wicked are the bless'd.

VI
Quoth John, our ign'rance is the cause
Why thus we blame our Maker's laws;
Parts of his ways alone we know,
'Tis all that man can see below.

VII
See'st thou that Carpet, not half done,
Which thou, dear Dick, hast well begun?
Behold the wild confusion there,
So rude the mass it makes one stare!

VIII
A stranger, ign'rant of the trade,
Wou'd say, no meaning's there convey'd;
For where's the middle, where's the border?
Thy Carpet now is all disorder.

IX
Quoth Dick, my work is yet in bits,
But still in every part it fits;
Besides, you reason like a lout,
Why, man, that *Carpet's inside out.*

X
Says John, thou say'st the thing I mean,
And now I hope to cure thy spleen;
This world, which clouds thy soul with doubt,
Is but a Carpet inside out.

XI
As when we view these shreds and ends,
We know not what the whole intends;
So when on earth things look but odd,
They're working still some scheme of God.

XII

No plan, no pattern can we trace,
All wants proportion, truth, and grace;
The motley mixture we deride,
Nor see the beauteous upper side.

XIII

But when we reach that world of light,
And view these works of God aright;
Then shall we see the whole design,
And own the workman is divine.

XIV

What now seem random strokes, will there
All order and design appear;
Then shall we praise what here we spurn'd,
For then the *Carpet shall be turn'd*.

XV

Thou'rt right, quoth Dick, no more I'll grumble,
That this sad world's so strange a jumble;
My impious doubts are put to flight,
For my own Carpet sets me right.

Hannah More, *Cheap Repository Tracts*, Vol II, (1796)

6 The Education of Apprentices

In 1802 a Bill regulating the working conditions of apprentices was passed. One of the Act's requirements was that apprentices be provided with free part-time education.

... VI. And be it further enacted, That every such Apprentice shall be instructed, in some Part of every working Day, for the First Four Years at least of his or her Apprenticeship, which shall next ensue from and after the Second Day of *December* One thousand eight hundred and two, if he or she is an Apprentice on the said Second Day of *December* One thousand eight hundred and two, and for the First Four Years at least of his or her Apprenticeship, if his or her Apprenticeship commences at any Time after the said Second Day of *December* one thousand eight hundred and two, in the usual Hours of Work, in Reading, Writing, and Arithmetick, or either of them, according to the Age and Abilities of such Apprentice, by some discreet and proper Person, to be provided and paid by the Master or Mistress of such Apprentice, in some Room or Place in such Mill or Factory to be set apart for that Purpose; and that the Time hereby directed to be allotted for such Instruction as aforesaid, shall be deemed and taken on all Occasions as Part of the respective Periods limited by this Act during which any such Apprentice shall be employed or compelled to work.

VII. And be it further enacted, That the Room or Apartment in which any Male Apprentice shall sleep, shall be entirely separate and distinct from the Room or Apartment in which any Female Apprentice shall sleep; and that not more than Two Apprentices shall in any Case sleep in the same Bed.

VIII. And be it further enacted, That every Apprentice, or (in case the Apprentices shall attend in Classes), every such Class shall, for the Space of One Hour at least every *Sunday*, be instructed and examined in the Principles of the Christian Religion, by some proper Person to be provided and paid by the Master or Mistress of such Apprentice; and in *England* and *Wales*, in case the Parents of such Apprentice shall be Members of the Church of *England*, then such Apprentice shall be taken, Once at least in every Year during the Term of his or her Apprenticeship, to be examined by the Rector, Vicar, or Curate of the Parish in which such Mill or Factory shall be situate; and shall also after such Apprentice shall have attained the Age of Fourteen Years, and before attaining the Age of Eighteen Years, be duly instructed and prepared for Confirmation, and be brought or sent to the Bishop of the Diocese to be confirmed, in case any Confirmation shall, during such Period, take Place in and for the said Parish; and in *Scotland* where the Parents of such Apprentice shall be Members of the Established Church, such Apprentice shall be taken, Once at least in every Year, during the Term of his or her Apprenticeship, to be examined by the Minister of the Parish; and shall after such Apprentice shall have attained the Age of Fourteen Years, and before attaining the Age of Eighteen Years, be carried to the Parish Church to receive the Sacrament of the Lord's Supper, as the same is administered in Churches in *Scotland*; and such Master or Mistress shall send all his or her Apprentices under the Care of some proper Person, Once in a Month at least, to attend during Divine Service in the Church of the Parish or Place in which the Mill or Factory shall be situated, or in some other convenient Church or Chapel where Service shall be performed according to the Rites of the Church of *England*, or according to the established Religion in *Scotland*, as the Case may be, or in some licensed Place of Divine Worship; and in case the Apprentices of any such Master or Mistress cannot conveniently attend such Church or Chapel every *Sunday*, the Master or Mistress, either by themselves or some proper Person, shall cause Divine Service to be performed in some convenient Room or Place in or adjoining to the Mill or Factory, Once at least every *Sunday* that such Apprentices shall not be able to attend Divine Service at such Church or Chapel; and such Master or Mistress is hereby strictly enjoined and required to take due Care that all his or her Apprentices regularly attend Divine Service, according to the Directions of this Act. An Act for the Preservation of the Health and Morals of Apprentices and others, employed in Cotton and other Mills, and Cotton and other Factories. 42 Geo III, c 73

7 Samuel Whitbread's Parochial Schools Bill

Samuel Whitbread (1758–1815), Member of Parliament for Bedford, introduced a Bill which provided two years free education for every child, financed from the poor rate. The Bill was given a second reading in a sparsely attended House, and was eventually thrown out by the House of Lords. This debate illustrates the range of views on the subject.

――――――

[PAROCHIAL SCHOOLS BILL.] Mr. *Whitbread* moved the second reading of the Parochial Schools bill. The question being put,

Mr. *Davies Giddy* rose and said, that while he was willing to allow the hon. gent. who brought forward this bill, every degree of credit for the goodness of his intentions, as well as for his ability and assiduity; still, upon the best consideration he was able to give the bill, he must totally object to its principle, as conceiving it to be more pregnant with mischief than advantage to those for whose advantage it was intended, and for the country in general. For, however specious in theory the project might be, of giving education to the labouring classes of the poor, it would, in effect, be found to be prejudicial to their morals and happiness; it would teach them to despise their lot in life, instead of making them good servants in agriculture, and other laborious employments to which their rank in society had destined them; instead of teaching them subordination, it would render them factious and refractory, as was evident in the manufacturing counties; it would enable them to read seditious pamphlets, vicious books, and publications against Christianity; it would render them insolent to their superiors; and, in a few years, the result would be, that the legislature would find it necessary to direct the strong arm of power towards them, and to furnish the executive magistrates with much more vigorous laws than were now in force. Besides, if the bill were to pass into a law, it would go to burthen the country with a most enormous and incalculable expence, and to load the industrious orders of society with still heavier imposts. It might be asked of him, would he abolish the Poor-Laws altogether? He had no hesitation to declare he would; for, although they relieved many persons, who were certainly objects of compassion, they were also abused by contributing to the support of idleness and profligacy; and he never could admit it to be just or reasonable that the labour of the industrious man should be taxed to support the idle vagrant. This was taxing virtue for the maintenance of vice. He concluded by moving, that the bill be read a second time this day three months.

Mr. *Morris* concurred in opinion with the hon. gent., though he was not prepared to go the full length of all his objections. He agreed, that the establishment of a system so universal, must entail upon the country an incalculable expence, at least 2s. in the pound upon the poor's rates; and he thought, that as a national system of education, the expence should rather be paid out of the Consolidated Fund, than by a local assessment upon parishes. In Scotland, he said, the public charge upon the country was but 6000*l.* a year for allowances to schoolmasters for the poor, while the remainder was made up by charges upon the landlord and tenant, or by voluntary subscription; while in England, a single charitable society for propagating Gospel knowledge, expended 4000*l.* a year, being two thirds of the whole public charge in Scotland.

Mr. *Ellison* gave great credit to the hon. gent. who brought in this bill, as well for his good intention in bringing it forward, as for his care in circulating it for the consideration of the magistrates throughout the kingdom. It had been fully considered; but every magistrate with whom he had conversed, was decidedly averse to it, and instructed their representatives to oppose it. He was convinced the operation of the poor-laws and the public charitable schools, already in existence, were fully adequate to ameliorate the situation of the poor. But if there were schools to be built, provided under this bill, and schoolmasters and mistresses employed in 14,000 parishes, the expence must be enormous.

Mr. *S. Bourne* wished the bill should stand over to the next session. And he begged, in the mean time, to suggest to the hon. gent. who brought it forward, that it would perhaps be better not to make the bill compulsory upon all parishes, but merely to enable the overseers, with the consent of the vestry in any parish, to raise, by way of rate, a sum for the support of schools, which they were not enabled to do as the law now stood; voluntary education was at all times preferable to compulsory; and some measure of this kind, he conceived, would prove more effectual than the present. He must add, also, that the situation of parish apprentices demanded the attention of the house. Almost every magistrate must have heard of cases of atrocity, with regard to their treatment, that ought, if possible, to be prevented. They were to be imputed principally to the compulsory nature of the obligation to take them.

Sir *Samuel Romilly* lamented the very different reception this bill met with now, compared with what it had experienced in the last parliament. He thought the bill ought to be allowed to go into a committee, where it might receive full consideration, and such amendments as might give it a fair chance of going forth to the country in a form less liable to objections. An hon. gent. complained that the poor-laws were abused for the maintenance of profligates; but it was the very object of this bill to render the poor less profligate, and less in need of eleemosynary support. He agreed with the last speaker as to the importance of attending to the condition of parish apprentices. It was the practice to send them to as great a distance as possible, where they had no friends who could attend to their situation. In some parishes in London they were accustomed to send them to the distance of some hundreds of miles, and to contract with the proprietors of the cotton mills of Lancashire, etc. for so many of them, who were sent off in carts like so many negro slaves.

Mr. *Rose* would be sorry to oppose the bill going into a committee, provided it was understood it should not pass this session. He had no doubt that the poor ought to be taught to read; as to writing, he had some doubt, because those who had learnt to write well, were not willing to abide at the plough, but looked to a situation in some counting house. With respect to the poor-rates, if they did not now exist, he would propose them, because he thought that the relief of the poor ought not to be left with the generous to the exemption of the miser.

Mr. *Lushington* supported the principle of the bill, and argued for going into a committee. In every country where the poor were well instructed, they formed the better subjects in every point of view. This measure would rather diminish than increase the poor-rates.

Mr. *R. Dundas* felt the strongest predilection for parochial schools, and certainly agreed in the principle of extending information as much as possible among the lower ranks. The object however, for which he rose, was to state in answer to the hon. and learned gent. over the way (Mr. Morris), that the expence was greater in Scotland, than what he supposed it to be. The rates for the schools there, were levied on the landlords, who resorted to their tenants for one half; they besides settled a rate of fees from such of the landlords as could pay them.

Mr. *Simeon* was decidedly against the bill, as going to inflict a compulsory education on the country at a most incalculable expence. At all events he thought that a bill of so much importance to every part of the country, ought not to be discussed in so thin a house, and in the absence of the magistrates and country gentlemen, who were the persons competent to throw the most light on the subject.

Lord *Milton* expressed his surprise that any objection should be thrown in the way of the bill in this stage of it. He replied to the argument, that those who had got some education would look higher, because they were above the generality. This would not be the case if the generality of the lower orders were well educated. There must be a lower order of people who must perform the manual labour of a country; and the better informed they were, the better they would be in every respect.

Mr. *Wharton*, in answer to the last speaker, begged leave to ask, whether the noble lord would have the ministers and churchwardens hold a critical examination in order to ascertain who were fit to be exalted to the counting-house, and who were only fit for the plough?

Mr. *Whitbread* replied, that the hon. gent., with his examinations, had chosen to attach a meaning to his noble friend's words that had never entered his head. His noble friend had

intimated that there must be a lower order, and the better informed they were, the better they would be. There would be no
need of the hon. gent.'s examination. The thing would settle itself. With respect to the arguments about the absence of
country gentlemen, and the thinness of the attendance, they
had no weight whatever with him. There were questions which
interested the passions of men, on which there would be a great
attendance; there were others of the last importance, of which
he considered the present as one, on which the attendance
would always be thin. He meant to persevere, in order to have a
decision on the grand principle, and he would not put off the
matter when there were occurrences arising day after day fully
sufficient to occupy the time that could be spared on any future
occasion. If the matter was not considered when it was fresh in
the mind, it would not be considered at all. All the arguments
for postponing it were therefore futile in the highest degree. If
the matter were to lie over for ten years, it would not be considered till it was pressed forward. What he wanted at present
was to have this grand question decided, "whether it was proper
that education should be diffused among the lower classes, or
not?" That the principle was sound, he was convinced; whether
the country was ripe for it, was another question. That it would
be adopted some time or other, he had no doubt; if it was rejected at present, he could only conclude that the country was
not yet ripe for it. As to the abolition of the poor-rates, that was
at present out of the question. As to the expence of education, it
was stated by many at a great deal more than it would actually
amount to. All the lower orders had an education of some sort,
good or bad. It had been said that it might be as well to teach
them to play on the fiddle, or to be skilful boxers. This practice
of boxing, by-the-bye, as a mode of settling differences, he
thought ought not to be discouraged, because it was much
better than the stiletto. But a fiddler or boxer would not be the
worse for being able to write and read. At St. Giles's there was
an education; children were taught to pick pockets, and to go
on from one degree of dexterity in wickedness to another, till

c

they came to the gallows; and most of the unhappy creatures
who perished there, were such as were unable to read or write.
He adverted to the too great severity of our criminal code,
which he was convinced had not the effect of diminishing the
number of crimes. Among the society called Quakers, crime
was almost unknown, and this was accounted for by their being
educated in their earliest years. The expence here would be
greater, it was said, than in Scotland. But Scotland was not so
large nor so opulent. He denied that the people, if generally
educated, would be averse to continue at the plough. On the
contrary, the ground would be better tilled, masters better
served, etc. The hon. gent. then replied to the argument about
their reading political pamphlets. When a riotous mob was
assembled, it was called an illiterate mob. If one man had
knowledge, he would have a much better chance of leading a
thousand ignorant creatures to mischief, than if they were all so
far informed as to read what might appear on both sides of the
question. He then begged the house to look at the situation of
Ireland. There the combinations were formed by the ignorant,
where their ignorance made them the dupes of the wicked. In
the three kingdoms, the excellence of the population would
appear to be in proportion to the degrees of information among
the lower classes. As to the vices of the lower orders, which had
been mentioned by an hon. gent., vices certainly did prevail
more or less everywhere; but in those places where the lower
orders were most remarkable for their vices the example was set
them by their superiors, who were generally more vicious than
they. It was said that the effect of the bill would be to impose an
additional rate of a shilling in the pound. He answered, no. It
was said, it would do away charities. It would do no such thing.
His aim was, to provide schools and school-masters where they
were wanted; where they were not, the magistrates would have
the power to suspend the operation of the law. The business
was committed to the magistrates, who were the most proper
persons to carry the act into execution. The system of magi-
stracy had defects; but in what other country was there a body

so excellent? As to the suggestion of the hon. gent. (Mr. S. Bourne), he thought that his own was the best plan; but, however, he would rather adopt his voluntary mode than none at all. He had done his duty in bringing this bill forward; and he should persevere until the house should divide upon it; and if they were to reject it, he should nevertheless go away, convinced of its utility, and conscious that it was rejected only because the house was not ripe for its adoption.

The Marquis of *Titchfield* thought much benefit might result from general education, but said that benefit might cost too dear. He wished therefore for some information as to the probable expence.

Mr. *Whitbread* could not say how far the parishes might be provided with, or be destitute of buildings that might answer for schools. In many parishes it would not be necessary to expend a shilling on that account. School-masters could be provided at a very cheap rate.

The *Chancellor of the Exchequer* wished the bill to go into a committee, with a view to the utmost fairness of consideration. It was the wish, unquestionably, of every one in the house to render the lower classes of the community better and happier. He feared however, that the kind of education here proposed, though it might give learning, would not contribute much to diffuse industry, religion, or morality. He feared a general legislative establishment would injure and destroy the voluntary establishments for public education now existing. He recommended a commission of enquiry to ascertain the state of charitable foundations for public education already established. A commission of that kind was now prosecuting a similar investigation in Ireland without any salary to the commissioners, and with but very few clerks. When such a commission should have ascertained what had been already done, it would be time enough to enquire what further might be done. He defended the principle of the poor-laws. However the system might be abused, as every large system must be liable to abuse, it was a proud characteristic of the nation, that charity was incorporated into the legislature. The poor of this country had consequently an interest in the maintenance of its constitution and independence, which the poor of no other country had. He said the education proposed would disqualify the persons possessing it from the most necessary, and useful description of labour. The Quakers were mentioned as a class universally educated. The example strengthened his argument; for he never knew of an Agricultural Quaker. He wished the bill to be made as perfect as possible, though he did not think it advisable ultimately to adopt it, and without a prospect of ultimate adoption it would perhaps be useless labour to improve the plan.

Mr. *Shaw Lefevre* vindicated the criminal code by the many instances of the royal mercy that appeared on different occasions.

Mr. *Whitbread* said, that the instances of the royal mercy were the best proof of what he had said.

Sir *John Newport* contended, that the code was sanguinary, and that experience had shewn that capital punishment could not annihilate the crime of forgery. He contended, that the commutation of death, the effect of which was momentary, to some other punishment, under a prolonged life of labour and degradation, would be much more effectual than the gallows. —The gallery was then cleared; but it was agreed that the bill should be read a second time without a division. When strangers were admitted,

Sir *T. Turton* spoke in favour of going into the committee, but he thought compulsory education unadviseable, when voluntary education was every-where establishing itself so extensively.

Mr. *Simeon* saw no good that could arise from going into a committee, and therefore opposed the speaker's leaving the chair, on the same grounds that he had objected to the second reading.

Mr. *Spencer Stanhope* informed the house, that he had been instructed by the magistrates of a very large and populous city to oppose the bill; in fact, he had reason to suppose that the majority of the magistrates and other principal inhabitants throughout the north of England were averse to the measure. The opposition which the hon. member made to the bill, he rested principally on the ground of the difficulty which existed as to our obtaining a sufficient number of schoolmasters, and on the impracticability of compulsory education.

Lord *Henry Petty* expressed his difference in opinion from those gentlemen who apprehended that danger might result from carrying the education of the lower orders too far, as they expressed it. The measure which was then before the house went no farther than barely to furnish youth who were destitute of all other means, with a certain source of obtaining a very plain and limited education. The magistrates in the north objected to this measure, he understood, on an apprehension that they would be compelled to erect schools, and go to other expence, which would be in many parts unnecessary, as they already possessed within themselves sufficient means of education for the children of the poor in that part of the country. It was to be observed, however, that there was a clause in the bill expressly for the purpose of preventing the extension of its operations to places in which there might be already establishments formed adequate to the purposes of the bill. If it should be found, however, that the bill was not sufficiently strong in that respect, any emendation on that head would be best effected when the bill should be in a committee.—Mr. Whitbread and Mr. D. Giddy said a few words in explanation, after which, the house divided; when the numbers were,

> For going into a committee 47
> Against it 13
> —
> Majority 34

Hansard's *Parliamentary Debates*, First series, Vol IX, col 798–806 (13 July 1807)

8 Joseph Lancaster Improvements in Education

The monitorial system devised by Joseph Lancaster (1778–

1838) was applied in those schools sponsored by the non-conformist British and Foreign School Society. Lancaster was particularly concerned with keeping down costs.

A Method of teaching to spell and read, whereby one Book will serve instead of Six Hundred Books

It will be remembered, that the usual mode of teaching requires every boy to have a book: yet, each boy can only read or spell one lesson at a time, in that book. Now, all the other parts of the book are in wear, and liable to be *thumbed* to pieces; and, whilst the boy is learning a lesson in one part of the book, the other parts are at that time useless. Whereas, if a spelling book contains twenty or thirty different lessons, and it were possible for thirty scholars to read the thirty lessons in that book, it would be equivalent to thirty books for its utility. To effect this, it is desirable the whole of the book should be printed three times larger than the common size type, which would make it equal in size and cost to three common spelling books, value from eight-pence to a shilling each. Again, it should be printed with only one page to a leaf, which would again double the price, and make it equivalent in bulk and cost to five or six common books; its different parts should then be pasted on pasteboard, and suspended by a string, to a nail in the wall, or other convenient place: one paste-board should contain the alphabet; others, words and syllables of from two to six letters. The reading lessons gradually rising from words of one syllable, in the same manner, till they come to words of five or six letters, or more, preparatory to the Testament lessons. There is a circumstance very seldom regarded enough, in the introductory lessons which youth usually have to perform before they are admitted to read in the Testament. A word of six letters or more, being di-vi-ded by hy-phens, reduces the syllables, which compose it to three, four, or five letters each; of course, it is as easy to read syllables, as words of five letters: and the child, who can read or spell the one, will find the other as easily attainable.

In the Testament, the words of two and three syllables are

undivided, which makes this division of the lessons a more natural introduction to the Testament. In the preparatory lessons I have used, the words are thus di-vi-ded.

When the cards are provided, as before mentioned, from twelve to twenty boys may stand in a circle round each card, and clearly distinguish the print, to read or spell, as well or better than if they had a common spelling book in each of their hands. If one spelling book was divided into thirty different parts or lessons, and each lesson given to a different boy, it would only serve thirty boys, changing their lessons among themselves, as often as needful; and the various parts would be continually liable to be lost or torn. But, every lesson placed on a card, will serve for twelve or twenty boys at once: and, when that twelve or twenty have repeated the whole lesson, as many times over as there are boys in the circle, they are dismissed to their spelling on the slate, and another like number of boys may study the same lesson, in succession: indeed, *two hundred boys* may all repeat their lessons from *one* card, in the space of *three hours*. If the value and importance of this plan, for saving paper and books in teaching reading and spelling, will not recommend itself, all I can say in its praise, from experience, will be of no avail. When standing in circles, to read or spell, the boys wear their numbers, tickets, pictures, etc. as described under the head, Emulation and Reward; and give place to each other, according to merit, as mentioned in the account of the two first classes. Joseph Lancaster. *Improvements in Education* (3rd ed 1805), 55–7

---

9 Rev Sydney Smith Mrs Trimmer and Joseph Lancaster

Mrs Sarah Trimmer (1741–1810) was well known as an author of children's books, and as the editor of the *Guardian of Education*. In 1805, in *A Comparative View of the New Plan of Education as promulgated by Mr. Joseph Lancaster*, she argued that his system was educationally unsound and a danger to the Established Church. For good measure, she accused him of stealing Bell's ideas. Not all Anglicans accepted her charges and the Rev Sydney Smith (1739–1827) wrote this scathing if laboured review of her book.

This is a book written by a lady who has gained considerable reputation at the corner of St Paul's Church-yard; who flames in the van of Mr Newberry's shop; and is, upon the whole, dearer to mothers and aunts than any other author who pours the milk of science into the mouths of babes and sucklings. Tired, at last, of scribbling for children, and getting ripe in ambition, she has now written a book for grown up people, and selected for her antagonist as stiff a controversialist as the whole field of dispute could well have supplied. Her opponent is Mr Lancaster, a Quaker, who has lately given to the world new and striking lights upon the subject of education, and come forward to the notice of his country by spreading order, knowledge, and innocence among the lowest of mankind.

Mr Lancaster, she says, wants method in his book; and therefore her answer to him is without any arrangement. The same excuse must suffice for the desultory observations we shall make upon this lady's publication.

The first sensation of disgust we experienced at Mrs Trimmer's book, was from the patronizing and protecting air with which she speaks of some small part of Mr Lancaster's plan. She seems to suppose, because she has dedicated her mind to the subject, that her opinion must necessarily be valuable upon it; forgetting it to be barely possible, that her application may have made her more wrong, instead of more right. If she can make out her case, that Mr Lancaster is doing mischief in so important a point as that of national education, she has a right, in common with every one else, to lay her complaint before the public; but a right to publish praises must be earned by something more difficult that the writing sixpenny books for children. They may be very good; though we never remember to have seen any one of them: but if they be no more remarkable for judgment and discretion than parts of the work before us, there are many thriving children quite capable of repaying the obligations they owe to their amiable instructress, and of teaching, with grateful retaliation, 'the *old* idea how to shoot.'

In remarking upon the work before us, we shall exactly follow the plan of the authoress, and prefix, as she does, the titles of those subjects on which her observations are made; doing her the justice to presume that her quotations are fairly taken from Mr Lancaster's book.

Mr Lancaster's Preface. —Mrs Trimmer here contends, in opposition to Mr Lancaster, that ever since the establishment of the Protestant Church, the education of the poor has been a national concern in this country; and the only argument she produces in support of this extravagant assertion, is an appeal to the act of uniformity. If there are millions of Englishmen who cannot spell their own names, or read a sign-post which bids them turn to the right or left, is it any answer to this deplorable ignorance to say, there is an act of parliament for public instruction?—to shew the very line and chapter where the King, Lords, and Commons, in Parliament assembled, ordain the universality of reading and writing—when, centuries afterwards, the ploughman is no more capable of the one or the other than the beast which he drives? In point of fact there is no Protestant country in the world where the education of the poor has been so grossly and infamously neglected as in England. Mr Lancaster has the very high merit of calling the public attention to this evil, and of calling it in the best way, by new and active remedies; and this uncandid and feeble lady, instead of using the influence she has obtained over the anility of these realms, to join that useful remonstrance which Mr Lancaster has begun, pretends to deny that the evil exists; and when you ask where are the schools, rods, pedagogues, primmers, histories of Jack the Giant-killer, and all the usual apparatus for education, the only thing she can produce is *the act of uniformity and common prayer.* . . . [Here follows a detailed defence of Lancaster's teaching methods.]

. . . The main object, however, for which this book is written, is to prove that the church establishment is in danger, from the increase of Mr Lancaster's institutions. Mr Lancaster is, as we have before observed, a Quaker. As a Quaker, he says, I cannot teach your creeds; but I pledge myself not to teach my own. I pledge myself (and if I deceive you, desert me, and give me up) to confine myself to those points of Christianity in which all Christians agree. To which Mrs Trimmer replies, that, in the first place, he cannot do this; and, in the next place, if he did do it, it would not be enough. But why, we would ask, cannot Mr Lancaster effect his first object? The practical and the feeling parts of religion, are much more likely to attract the attention, and provoke the questions of children, than its speculative doctrines. A child is not very likely to put any questions at all to a catechizing master, and still less likely to lead him into subtle and profound disquisition. It appears to us not only practicable, but very easy, to confine the religious instruction of the poor, in the first years of life, to those general feelings and principles which are suitable to the established church, and to every sect; afterwards, the discriminating tenets of each subdivision of Christians may be fixed upon this general basis. To say that this is not enough, that a child should be made an Antisocinian, or an Antipelagian, in his tenderest years, may be very just; but what prevents you from making him so? Mr Lancaster, purposely and intentionally to allay all jealousy, leaves him in a state as well adapted for one creed as another. Begin; make your pupil a firm advocate for the peculiar doctrines of the English church; dig round about him, on every side, a trench that shall guard him from every species of heresy. In spite of all this clamour, you do nothing; you do not stir a single step; you educate alike the swineherd and his hog;—and then, when a man of real genius and enterprise rises up, and says, let me dedicate my life to this neglected object; I will do every thing but that which must necessarily devolve upon you alone;—you refuse to do your little; and compel him, by the cry of Infidel and Atheist, to leave you to your antient repose, and not to drive you, by insidious comparisons, to any system of active utility.

We deny, again and again, that Mr Lancaster's instruction is any kind of impediment to the propagation of the doctrines of the church; and if Mr Lancaster was to perish with his system to-morrow, these boys would positively be taught nothing; the doctrines which Mrs Trimmer considers to be prohibited would not rush in, but there would be an absolute vacuum. We will, however, say this in favour of Mrs Trimmer, that if every one who has joined in her clamour, had laboured one hundredth part as much as she has done in the cause of national education, the clamour would be much more rational, and much more consistent, than it now is. By living with a few people as active as herself, she is perhaps somehow or another persuaded that there is a national education going on in this country. But our principal argument is, that Mr Lancaster's plan is at least better than the *nothing* which preceded it. The authoress herself seems to be a lady of respectful opinions, and very ordinary talents; defending what is right without judgement, and believing what is holy without charity. *Edinburgh Review*, Vol IX (October 1806), 177–84

PART TWO

The Voluntary Societies

The establishment in 1808 of the non-sectarian Royal Lancasterian Institution (later known as the British and Foreign School Society) marked a significant development in the history of education. It was the first of a variety of voluntary educational societies, via which working-class children were to receive an education over the next sixty years (10). Three years later, in 1811, the Anglican church established the National Society for Promoting the Education of the Poor in the Principles of the Established Church—its motives evident in the name it chose for itself (11). The National Society was able to call on the support of parishes throughout England and Wales, and rapidly became the most important educational body in the land. But not all poor children, nor even a majority, attended the schools organised by these voluntary bodies, and a great many, particularly children in the London area, had no day schooling of any kind (12). For a very few there was educational provision of exceptional quality in schools like Robert Owen's at New Lanark (13).

The voluntary societies had many problems, not least that of the quality of their teachers. Many of these had little formal education themselves, and few had professional training as teachers. To assist them, and to ensure that they followed the syllabus determined by the societies, carefully prepared teacher manuals (14), textbooks and question-and-answer books were devised (15).

10 The British and Foreign School Society Manifesto

The Royal Lancasterian Institution for the Education of the Poor (which later became the British and Foreign School Society) was founded in 1808. It proposed to provide a non-sectarian education, and Anglicans as well as nonconformists were on the committee.

ADDRESS
OF
THE COMMITTEE
FOR PROMOTING
THE ROYAL LANCASTERIAN SYSTEM
FOR THE EDUCATION OF THE POOR

The present address is made to those who, possessing the common feelings of humanity, wish to see all the good bestowed upon the lower orders of their species, of which their place in society admits. To all those who are not strangers to so humane a sentiment, it is an invitation to ask their own reason, whether the education of the poor is not an advantage of this description; and to afford us their aid, if we can prove to them that it will be attended with the most beneficial effects.

We present to their consideration a plan for extending to the poor the knowledge of reading, writing, and common arithmetic, more efficacious, and more economical in respect to both time and money, than has hitherto been conceived to be within the sphere of possibility. It is a plan which, while it calls upon the superior and middling classes for nothing that admits the name of a sacrifice, promises to bestow upon them more able and more trust-worthy associates in all the circumstances of life, in which we are dependent upon the co-operation and fidelity of our subordinate brethren. It is probably not sufficiently considered to what an extent that dependence reaches. The poor are our inmates and our guardians. They surround our tables, they surround our beds, they inhabit our nurseries. Our lives, our properties, the minds and the health of our children are to an inconceivable degree dependent upon their good or evil qualities.

According to the system which Mr. Lancaster has not only established, but already reduced to practice, and of the practical efficacy of which the most satisfactory experience has now been obtained, the children of the poor, before they are old enough to work, can be completely taught the valuable acquirements of reading, writing, and arithmetic, at an expense, even in the metropolis, of little more than five shillings per annum for each. It follows evidently from this most important fact, that by a combination requiring very slender efforts among the benevolent and public-spirited members of the community, those useful attainments may be extended to the whole of the rising generation, and the pious wish of the SOVEREIGN be fully accomplished, "that every poor child in the kingdom should be able to read the Bible."

The points of utility naturally connected with this event are of two kinds, and both in the highest degree important. The first respects the purposes to which the faculties in question might be turned in the different offices which devolve upon the lower orders. The second respects the frame of mind which is created during, and by the acquirement.

1. It is surely unnecessary to point out the innumerable modes in which the faculties of reading, writing and accounting, render the lower orders more useful coadjutors to us on those occasions in which we stand in need of their services; as domestics, as artisans, as manufacturers, as persons intrusted with the guardianship, the transfer, the improvement of our property in a thousand ways. It is impossible that any man capable of recalling to his mind the number and importance of these occasions, can doubt of the prodigious advantage derived to society from so great an addition to the useful faculties of the operative members of the community.

2. But, high as this advantage ought evidently to be ranked, it is still very inferior to that which arises from the frame of mind created by the *discipline* of education; by the habits of

order, and of the love of rational esteem, which it is its nature to engender. Let us but reflect upon the different modes in which the time required for education is spent by the children of the poor, when in a school like that of Mr. Lancaster's, and when at no school. If at no school, their time is for the most part at their own disposal; it is spent with idle companions like themselves, in all the disorderly courses of which idleness is the parent. Their life is (upon their own scale) an exact picture of that irregularity in the grown man, which produces almost all the unprofitable and dangerous members of society; and it cannot, from the known laws of the human constitution, operate otherwise than as a most fruitful seminary of this unhappy description of persons. In a school of Mr. Lancaster's, on the other hand, the children are inured to habits of order and subordination. They are delivered from idleness, and from the daring and disorderly courses for which it gives a taste. They become habituated to strive with one another for superiority in useful arts, and to look for praise from the attainment of real excellence. Who sees not that in the one course of training there is every chance of rearing valuable members of society? Who sees not that in the other there is every chance of rearing pernicious ones?

For the particular methods pursued in Mr. Lancaster's plan of education, we must refer to his own publications. One regulation it is necessary to state. In order to obviate the scruples which parents and guardians attached to any particular form of christianity might feel with respect to the religious instruction imparted in Mr. Lancaster's schools; and in order to extend the benefits of his plan of education to all the religious denominations of the community, instead of confining them to one or a few, it is an inviolable law to teach nothing but what is the standard of belief to all christians, THE SCRIPTURES THEMSELVES. The children are not only taught to read the Bible, but are trained in the habit of reading it, and are left entirely to the explanations and commentaries which their parents or friends may think it their duty to give them at home.

In the Borough school alone 8000 children have been educated, whose parents were of the poorest description, and hitherto no instance has been noticed of any one of these children being since charged with a criminal offence in any court of justice.

The patronage which Mr. Lancaster has received, particularly from Their Majesties and the whole of the Royal Family, having contributed powerfully to the general adoption of his plans, schools are now established in every county of England; several have been erected in Scotland, and some in Ireland. As the advantages of the system are more generally experienced, more numerous applications continue to be made to Mr. Lancaster for assistance in the formation of schools; bringing along with them an additional burthen of expense, and a demand for more extended means. It is sufficiently evident, that, in order to disseminate in the most perfect manner the benefits of the scheme, persons completely trained in its practical details, are highly necessary to be employed in conducting the first operations of every newly-erected seminary. Among the youths who come under Mr. Lancaster's care, it is his object to select those who appear best calculated for his purpose, and to train them up to become school-masters and school-mistresses in the new establishments which are successively formed. The instances which have already appeared, of youths of fourteen or fifteen years of age conducting with almost the regularity of a machine, schools containing several hundreds of children, and imparting to them, with unexampled rapidity, the elements of education, afford the most gratifying proofs of the adaptation of the expedients to the great object in view. The maintenance, however, of the young persons intended for this office, during the time of their preparation, has been experienced to be the grand source of expense attending this institution, reaching far beyond the unaided exertions of any individual to supply. . . .

Report of the Finance Committee and Trustees of The Royal Lancasterian Institution for The Education of the Poor, for the year 1811 (1812)

11 The National Society's Plan of Union

The Anglican organisation, the National Society for Promoting the Education of the Poor in the Principles of the Established Church, was founded in 1811. It sought to establish a day school in every parish in England and Wales.

PLAN OF UNION

The General Committee of the National Society having taken into their consideration, this day, a Plan of Union between the Diocesan and District Committees or Schools with the parent Society, came to the following Resolutions:—

That, whereas the establishment of such Committees and Schools is the principal mean by which the Society purposes and hopes to carry into effect the great end and design for which it has been formed, the Society is desirous of forwarding the progress of them by connecting them with itself, and by such assistance as the present means of the Society will allow.

That the foundation of this union between Diocesan and District Committees and Schools, with the parent Society, being understood to be a general conformity, on their part, with the principles on which the Society itself is constituted;

Therefore, for the purpose of giving assurance of such conformity, the Plan of such Committees and Schools, shall be, in the first instance, transmitted to the Diocesan, or District Committee, if there be any, and from thence to this Society, through its Secretary; or immediately to this Society, where there shall be no Diocesan or District Committee; and that, afterwards, annual, or, if desired, more frequent communications be made, in like manner, of their state and progress.

That in such Dioceses as have already, in conformity with the designs of the Society, formed Central Committees, under the superintendence of the respective Bishops, with which subordinate Schools correspond, it is recommended that the communications to this Society respecting the state and progress, as well of the Central as the subordinate Schools, be made from such Central Committees only; and that the same course and

D

order be observed in every other Diocese, in which a Central Committee may be formed, subsequent to the establishment of local Schools.

That it be also recommended, that wherever funds for the establishment of Schools are provided, or, in the way of being provided, such Schools be formed without delay.

That it is the wish and intention of the National Society to render, from time to time, pecuniary aid to the Diocesan and District Societies, as far as may be in its power.

That it will also assist them in procuring books, and a Master, for their Central School, at its first establishment; recommending, at the same time, that all Diocesan and District Societies once established, shall endeavour, as far as possible, to provide for the wants of *all* the Schools under their superintendence; and, for that purpose, shall establish a proper collection of books, and train up Teachers.

That the Society itself being instituted principally for Educating the Poor in the Doctrine and Discipline of the Established Church, according to the excellent Liturgy and Catechism provided for that purpose, it is required that all the Children received into these Schools be, without exception, instructed in this Liturgy and Catechism, and that, in conformity with the directions in that Liturgy, the Children of each School do constantly attend Divine Service, in their Parish Church, or other place of public worship, under the Establishment, wherever the same is practicable, on the Lord's Day; unless such reason for their non-attendance be assigned, as shall be satisfactory to the persons having the direction of that School: and that no religious tracts be admitted into any School but which are, or shall be contained in the Catalogue of the Society for Promoting Christian Knowledge.

T. T. WALMSLEY, Sec.

First Report of the National Society (1812), 27–8

___

12 William Allen   London schools

William Allen (1770–1843), Quaker philanthropist and

treasurer of the British and Foreign School Society, helped
found a school in Spitalfields. Here he describes for the
Select Committee of 1816 the inadequacies of London's
educational provisions.

Are you acquainted with the establishment of the school in
Spitalfields?—I was concerned in the first foundation of it. In
the course of the proceedings of the soup committees established
to assist the poor during seasons of scarcity, it occurred that the
same class of individuals who superintended that charity, would
extend their benevolent exertions to procure the means of
education for the objects of their care; this being suggested to
them, a special meeting of the committee was called, which
proceeded immediately to form a school society on the British
system, and to erect a school-house, which cost about 1,700*l*.
This school has already educated 2,000 children.

What year was it established in?—In the beginning of 1812.

How many can it educate?—If the children could be procured, it would contain full 800.

How many actually attend?—On an average 320.

What should you take to be the cause of the deficiency?—
One cause in that district, is the employment of the children in
the manufactures; but I have no doubt that if the school associations were made to operate, that the school would not only
be filled, but a necessity would appear for another being
established.

From what you know of the state of education in different
parts of the Metropolis, do you consider there are a great
number of poor children without the means of education?—
From what I have seen, which is principally founded upon the
investigation, which took place a few years ago, into the circumstance of fifteen hundred poor families in and about Spitalfields,
who received assistance from the soup institution, it appeared
that a great proportion of the parents were totally unable to
read; and I beg to state, that in some cases there was clear evidence of persons dying through scanty and insufficient food,

which brought on incurable maladies. The following is the general result of the investigation above alluded to.

[It was read.]

Can you form any estimate of the number of poor children in this Metropolis, who are without the means of education?—It is almost imposible to answer this question, until the inquiries now on foot shall be further advanced; but I have every reason to believe considerably more than 100,000. I beg this to be considered merely as a vague estimate, arising only from the opportunities that I have had of witnessing the want of education. I am confident that one half and upwards of the children of the poor are destitute of the means of education, and that a large proportion of them, through the neglect of society, are actually training in vice. *Select Committee on the Education of the Lower Orders*, 122–3, PP, 1816 (498), IV

_____

13 Robert Owen and the New Lanark School

Robert Owen (1771–1858), a social reformer, set up a school for the children of his employees at his New Lanark cotton mill. He considered that character was moulded at an early age by environment, and he endeavoured to provide a suitable educational environment for children at a modest cost. He explained his methods to the Select Committee in 1816.

_____

What is the plan adopted by you?—The children are received into a preparatory or training school at the age of three, in which they are perpetually superintended, to prevent them acquiring bad habits, to give them good ones, and to form their dispositions to mutual kindness and a sincere desire to contribute all in their power to benefit each other; these effects are chiefly accomplished by example and practice, precept being found of little use, and not comprehended by them at this early age; the children are taught also whatever may be supposed useful, that they can understand, and this instruction is combined with as much amusement as is found to be requisite for their health, and to render them active, cheerful and happy, fond of the school and of their instructors. The school, in bad weather, is held in apartments properly arranged for the purpose; but in fine weather the children are much out of doors, that they may have the benefit of sufficient exercise in the open air. In this training-school the children remain two or three years, according to their bodily strength and mental capacity; when they have attained as much strength and instruction as to enable them to unite, without creating confusion, with the youngest classes in the superior school, they are admitted into it; and in this school they are taught to read, write, account, and the girls, in addition, to sew; but the leading object in this more advanced stage of their instruction, is to form their habits and dispositions. The children generally attend this superior day school until they are ten years old; and they are instructed in healthy and useful amusements for an hour or two every day, during the whole of this latter period. Among these exercises and amusements, they are taught to dance; those who have good voices, to sing; and those among the boys who have a natural taste for music, are instructed to play on some instrument. At this age, both boys and girls are generally withdrawn from the day school, and are put into the mills or to some regular employment. Some of the children, however, whose parents can afford to spare the wages which the children could now earn, continue them one, two, or three years longer in the day school, by which they acquire an education which well prepares them for any of the ordinary active employments of life. Those children who are withdrawn from the day school at ten years of age, and put into the mills or to any other occupation in or near the establishment, are permitted to attend, whenever they like, the evening schools, exercises and amusements, which commence as from one to two hours, according to the season of the year, after the regular business of the day is finished, and continue about two hours; and it is found that out of choice about 400, on an average, attend every evening. During these two hours there is a regular change of instruction, and healthy exercise, all of which proceed with such order and regularity as to gratify every spectator, and leave no doubt on any mind, of the superior advantages to be derived from this combined system of instruction, exercise, and amusement. The 400 now mentioned are exclusive of 300 who are taught during the day. On the Sunday, the day scholars attend the school an hour and half in the morning and about the same time in the afternoon; and the evening scholars, as well as their parents and other adults belonging to the establishment, attend in the evening, when either some religious exercises commence, or a lecture is read, and afterwards the regular business of the evening Sunday school begins. These proceedings seem to gratify the population in a manner not easily to be described, and, if stated much below the truth, would not be credited by many; inspection alone can give a distinct and comprehensive view of the advantages which such a system affords to all parties interested or connected with it.

How many masters have you in the day schools?—Generally ten or eleven; in the evening schools usually two or three more.

Is the expense of this institution considerable?—It is, apparently; but I do not know how any capital can be employed to make such abundant returns, as that which is judiciously expended in forming the character and directing the labour of the lower classes. I have made out a short statement of the expense of the instruction of the Institution at Lanark, and the expense of the instruction for 700 scholars, part taught in the day and part in the evening, supposing schools to be erected and furnished: One rector or superior master, at 250*l.* per annum; ten assistants, males and females, at 30*l.* each on the average; light, heat, and materials of all kinds, 150*l.*; making together 700*l.* or 20s. per year for each child, which if taken under tuition at three years old, and retained to the age of ten, would be 7*l.* each, for forming the habits, dispositions, and general character, and instruction in the elements of every branch of useful knowledge; which acquirements would be of more real value to the individual, and through him to the community, than any sum of money that at present it would be prudent to state. The expenses attending the exercise and amusements are all included. *Select Committee on the Education of the Lower Orders*, 240–1, PP, 1816 (498), IV

14 Dr Bell's System of Education

Dr Andrew Bell's *An Experiment in Education* was too difficult for many teachers. The National Society published a simplified version of this work in question and answer form to assist them.

QUESTIONS AND ANSWERS
ON
DR. BELL'S
SYSTEM OF EDUCATION

Question. WHAT is the first thing to be done in forming a School on the Madras, or Dr. Bell's System?

Answer. It is to be arranged into classes.

Q. By what method?

A. By dividing the children according to the knowledge they may have of reading, spelling, or their letters.

Q. How is the master to discover this?

A. By finding out who have been at the same school previously together, and what proficiency they have made, or if the number be small, he may examine them all himself.

Q. Of what number should the classes consist?

A. The best number is from 24 to 36, or in large schools to 40; but that is not always possible; 120 scholars may perhaps be divided into six classes, having respect, as near as may be, to equality of progress in forming each class.

Q. What is the next step?

A. To select teachers, that is, the officers and agents, from among the children themselves, who are to assist in the government and instruction of the School.

Q. From what classes are the teachers selected?

A. From the higher classes.

Q. How are they selected?

A. By the elective voices of the higher classes, and best boys in the school, who scarcely ever fail to find the boys most suited for the purpose. A short time will enable the master to discover whether a right choice has been made. He must change them till he has good ones. They are to be found, and on the choice of these teachers the whole will depend.

Q. How should the master instruct the teachers in their duty?

A. By getting them to attend him at first at extra hours.

Q. What should be the general character of the teachers?

A. They must not merely be forward in their learning, but they must be boys of activity and energy, of good temper, steady to one thing; of as much judgment and discrimination as you can expect at so young an age.

Q. What is the business of a teacher?

A. To hear his class their lessons; to keep the registers; to apportion the length of each lesson, unless it is before determined by the regular rules of the school. In short, under the eye of the master, to direct the whole proceedings of the class; for the order, behaviour, and improvement of which he must be responsible.

Q. What else is also considered the business of the teacher?

A. He is expected, in particular, to tell, whenever asked, the number in his class both present and absent, the number of lessons said, and how much time has been occupied in saying them.

Q. What other officer is appointed to each class?

A. An assistant teacher.

Q. How is he selected?

A. From a higher class: or the best boy in each class may be chosen; as circumstances may point out, or as the class may require particular attention.

Q. What is his business?

A. To assist the teacher in hearing the lessons, and in keeping order in the class; and in case of the teacher's absence, to take the whole management of it himself. Whenever the teacher leaves the class, if but for a moment, the assistant should take his office, and the head boy of the class that of the assistant.

Q. Who is placed over the teachers?

A. An usher, who is to be the most active and intelligent boy in the School. His business is to see that the teachers do their duty, to instruct them in it, if necessary; to see that the registers are rightly kept, and, in short, to issue, and to see executed all the orders of the master.

Q. What is the duty of the master?

A. His perpetual employment is to overlook the whole School, and give life and energy to every member of it. He inspects the classes one by one, and is occupied, wherever there is most occasion for his services, and where they will have the greatest effect. He is to encourage the diffident, the timid, and the backward; to check and repress the forward and presumptuous, to bestow just and ample commendation upon the diligent, attentive, and orderly, however dull their capacity, or slow their progress; to regulate the ambitious, rouse the slothful, and make the idle exert themselves; in short, to deal out praise and blame, encouragement and threatening, according to the temper, disposition, and genius of the scholar. He is occasionally to hear and instruct the classes himself, and far oftener to watch over the general order, seeing that his numerous agents are at their posts, and alert, (rather than acting himself,) and overlooking the teachers and assistants, while hearing their respective classes.

Q. To whom is the master accountable? . . .

. . . Q. If one part of a class is more imperfect than another, how may this be remedied?

A. The boys most backward may individually say their lessons, to the more forward, i.e. they may be divided into tutor and pupil, and the former is responsible for the progress of the latter.

Q. What is the ground-work of all precision, and never dispensed with, without giving rise to much error and neglect?

A. *The marked book.*

Q. To whom are the marked books confined?

A. To the teachers and assistant teachers.

Q. Who should preserve a copy of them?

A. The master.

Q. For what purpose?

A. For the inspection of the superintendents and visitors.

Q. What is the duty of the master with regard to the marked book?

A. In each class the master marks with pen and ink in the front of the teacher's book, when taken in hand, the number of the class, the teacher's name, the day of the month, the manner in which it is to be read, and whether for the first or second time, etc.

Q. What is the teacher's part in keeping the marked book?

A. The teacher marks with pencil the day of the month, at the place where the lesson begins, every morning; and also where each lesson ends, as it is successively given out, during the day.

Q. At the close of the school for the day, what is done?

A. The individual proficiency of each scholar, or the place which he holds in his class, and his absence from school, if that should happen, is entered in a register by the teachers, ushers, and other competent officers.

Q. What other register is kept?

A. *The register of business*, in which is inserted the sum of the daily tasks noted in the marked book, or performed during the day; the number of lessons read, pages or lines ended at, and hours thus employed, in three adjoining columns; and so with the catechism, religious instruction, writing, ciphering, etc. These are added weekly and monthly, and compared by the master and teachers with what was done the preceding day, week, and month.

Q. Of what particular benefit are the registers?

A. They are great instruments of discipline, and produce precision and exactness. Both to the master and visitor they afford the readiest means of ascertaining the progress, and present state of the school, and the regularity of attendance of each scholar. It is at one view thus shown what has been done during any given period by each class, and a trial will prove whether it has been gone over properly and correctly.

N.B. In Sunday Schools the register may be examined once in every month, and the progress of the children may be enquired into at any given period. This account should be kept by the masters of the schools at extra hours, as the time is limited when the school is held on Sundays alone. The process of instruction may be the same, but it would perhaps be advisable to have what is usually called, "the religious instruction," in the morning, and the reading in the afternoon.

Q. What mode would you take periodically to ascertain the progress of the children?

A. A weekly examination attended by the visitors and members of the Committee.

Q. In what way should such weekly examinations be conducted?

A. Each class should be brought up separately, and the teacher be desired to hear them, under the direction of the visitor, in the whole of the preceding week's business, or such part of it as the visitor may think proper, or out of any books they have previously gone through. Frederic Iremonger. *Dr. Bell's System of Instruction broken into short questions and answers for the use of Masters and Teachers in National Schools* (1825 ed)

15 Iremonger's Questions

The National Society produced a set of school readers for their schools, and to ensure that the readers were used in the proper manner they provided the teachers with suitable questions.

ADVERTISEMENT

In the following Compilation the Editor begs to acknowledge the assistance afforded him by the Rev. W. Whitear, the Rev. T. Bowdler, and the Rev. C. Pilkington, who have been long actively and practically engaged in carrying into effect the excellent designs of the National Society for the Education of the Poor. The want of such a manual has been strongly felt within their respective spheres of action, and many co-adjutors in the same cause have expressed their conviction of the utility of a publication of this description, particularly for Schools in smaller towns and country villages.

It should be fully understood, that the work is intended for the use of Masters and Teachers only; and it is admitted, that where the Visitors are constant in their attendance, and active in their exertions, the use of Printed Questions, for the Elementary Books, *may* be rendered unnecessary; still however it is to be feared that, in very many Schools, the admirable plan of questioning, so well calculated to call forth the attention and understanding of the Children, and thereby to fix permanently in their minds the instruction imparted to them, is at present very defective. In some instances no questions are asked; in others, improper ones; and the object of the Editor is solely to supply the want of a Questioning Book, where, under such circumstances, it may be felt. The children should be asked the questions the first time with their books open; afterwards their recollection should be exercised by trying them with their books shut. It would also be a profitable employment, if the Teacher was frequently to examine his class, by the Questioning Book, in the ground already gone over; and this examination should be without previous reading at the time. Thus when the Children are reading the 6th chapter of St. Matthew, they should be asked questions out of the 5th, etc.

In order still to leave some room for the exercise of the Teacher's judgment, it will be observed, that where the answers are to be given from the words of the book which the children are reading, they are not added in the present work; but merely where an explanation is required, and then they are to be learned by dictation from the mouth of the Teacher, in the same manner as the Catechism, or any other religious instruction. The Teacher should be satisfied, if the general sense is given, without being too particular as to the literal words.

QUESTIONS
FOR THE
DIFFERENT ELEMENTARY BOOKS,
ETC. ETC.

Questions for the National School Book, No. 2

... LES-SON VII.

The Bees, Drones, and Wasp.

When the drones went to a hive of bees, what did they do there?

What did they say?

Were the drones right or wrong in doing this?

Why so?

A. They should not have claimed what was not their own.

What did the bees do to the drones?

Who was to be the judge?

Why?

What did judge wasp say to them?

In whose hands did he tell them they had better place the cause?

What were they at the thought of this?

What did they give him?

In what way did he then tell them they had better decide the cause?

What did the *bees* do after he had thus spoken?

What did the *drones* do?

Upon this, how did judge wasp decide?

What is the lesson you learn from this story?

A. That it is foolish and wrong in any one to claim merit which he does not deserve.

How will it sooner or later be shewn whether his claim is just?

A. By his works.

LES-SON VII.

The Bees, Drones, and Wasp.

A set of drones went to a hive, where there was a swarm of bees, and laid claim to it; and said that the rich store and the combs were their goods. The bees went to law with them, and the wasp was to be judge of the cause, as one who well knew each one's right, and of course knew how to put an end to their suit. Friends, says he, the mode we use in these courts is so slow, and the suit costs so large a sum; but as you are both my friends, and I wish you well, I beg you will place the cause in my hands, and I will put an end to it in a short time. They were both glad at the thought of this, and in turn gave him thanks. Why then, that it may be seen who have a just claim to these rich combs, do you, says he to the bees, take this hive, and to the drones, do you take that, and go fill the cells as fast as you can, that we may know by the taste and look of it, who has the best claim in this cause. The bees then set to work, but the drones would not stand to it, and so judge Wasp gave the claim to the bees, and broke up the court.

Frederic Iremonger. *Questions for the Different Elementary Books used in the National Schools* (5th ed, 1826)

PART THREE

The Voluntary System Under Pressure

Sectarian rivalries would have presented a formidable obstacle had the British government attempted to intervene in education, but British administrators abroad had more freedom. In Ireland, a voluntary society linked with the British and Foreign School Society received an annual grant of several thousand pounds, starting in 1815 (16), and in 1831 the British government decided to establish a national system of education in that country (17)—a step not possible in England until 1870.

In England the campaign for state non-sectarian education gained momentum from the mid-1820s. The radicals and agnostics of various shades behind this movement (18) feared that as Britain was on the verge of a population explosion, it must, therefore, be on the verge of revolution. They argued that secular education of the masses was the way to avert catastrophe, and 'useful knowledge'—of which political economy was to be a major component (19)—should provide the basis of children's education. Teachers who had been struggling for years to work through a biblical syllabus saw the need for a wider education (20) and by the end of the 1830s the voluntary societies themselves came to accept the idea of a secularised curriculum (21).

Changes in the school curriculum were not matched by any marked developments in the monitorial system (22). Voluntary schools generally were not coping with the demands made of them, and the statistical societies' investigations give us some idea of the magnitude of the problems (23).

16 The Kildare Place Society

The British government was loth to interfere in English education but it had no such scruples in Ireland. From 1815 it gave an annual grant to the Society for Promoting the Education of the Poor in Ireland (popularly known as the Kildare Place Society). The Society established a teacher training school, appointed school inspectors, made grants towards teachers' salaries and school buildings, and prepared its own school books. Many of its innovations were later taken up by English and colonial educationists.

STATEMENT

THE Committee of this Society, anxious to make known its principles and objects, and to facilitate the intercourse between it and the Schools in correspondence with the Society, publishes the following Statement, divided into paragraphs for the facility of reference, and containing information and suggestions which may prove useful to all Schools for the Education of the Poor.

1. THIS Society is a voluntary Association of persons of various religious communions, formed for the purpose of diffusing the blessing of *well-ordered* Education amongst the labouring classes of this Country.

2. The leading principle on which it is pledged to act, is to afford the same facilities for Education to every denomination of Christians, without interfering with the peculiar religious opinions of any.

3. With this view the Society is anxious to promote the establishment and assist in the support of Schools, in which the appointment of Governors and Teachers, and the admission of Scholars, shall be uninfluenced by religious distinctions, and in which the Bible or Testament without note or comment, shall

be read by *all the Scholars who have attained a suitable proficiency in reading*, excluding catechisms and books of religious controversy; but the Society wish it to be distinctly understood, that the Bible or Testament is not to be used as a *School Book*, from which children are to be taught to spell or to read.

4. Such is the description of Schools which the Society conceives best adapted to *the wants and circumstances of this Country*; it is hoped, that in such Seminaries the labouring classes may obtain suitable instruction, without any attempt being made to disturb their religious opinions; and that the children of the poor being thus associated together without distinction, may thereby learn to regard each other without prejudice, and to indulge a charitable feeling for their neighbours, of whatever religious persuasion they may be.

5. But although an anxious consideration of the circumstances of this country, has convinced the Members of the Institution, that *particular* religious instruction ought not to be introduced into the Schools during school hours, yet the Society is fully sensible of the value of such instruction, as forming an indispensable branch of Education; and the mode of instruction recommended by the Society, gives a facility to the parents and pastors of the children, to impart to them such religious instruction as they may think fit, out of School hours.

6. In other respects the Society does not assume any control over the internal regulations of the Schools which it assists; but it *recommends* that such a system of instruction shall be adopted, as shall enable the Peasant and Artizan to obtain information *suited to their stations in life*, without encroaching materially on their time or their means;—that the morals of Pupils and Instructors shall be carefully attended to, and principles of truth and honesty inculcated:—that the children shall be accustomed to habits of decency and cleanliness; and that they shall be taught to fix their attention exclusively on whatever business they may be engaged in, and inured to that kind of regular

discipline and good order, which is of such essential value to all, and particularly to those who must earn their bread by their industry.

7. The Society has established a Model School in Dublin, on an extensive scale, which is intended to exemplify the system of Education recommended by the Society, and also to serve as a seminary for training Schoolmasters.

8. This seminary is open from the 15th October in each year, to the 1st of May in the following year, for the admission of all persons properly recommended, and desirous of learning the improved method of teaching, without any charge being made for tuition, and also without any condition being imposed as to the regulations of the Schools in which they may afterwards be engaged.

9. The time required to communicate sufficient information in this way, to a man who has been previously qualified to teach in the ordinary manner, is from six to eight weeks; and *where Masters are to be educated for Schools established on the principles recommended by the Society,* and their conduct while attending the Model School, shall be deserving of encouragement, the Society will allow a sum of money for the expenses of such persons, whilst travelling to and from Dublin; and during the period of their tuition, will maintain them in the Society's House, Kildare-Place.

10. As the most perfect system of instruction, must be of comparatively little value, where the Master is incompetent, the Society anxiously recommends that all persons desirous of having Schoolmasters of their own nomination, trained in the Seminary, should be exceedingly careful in the selection of the individuals for that purpose. Their age should not be less than eighteen, nor more than thirty years: they ought to have a competent knowledge of spelling, reading, writing, and arithmetic; in temper they should be patient; in disposition mild, but firm; of diligent habits; of unblemished moral character;

E

and fully convinced of the importance of inculcating on the young mind, a love of decency and cleanliness, of industry, honesty and truth.

11. No person can be admitted into the Training School, and *maintained at the expense of the Society*, who is over thirty-five years of age, nor until he shall have been examined by the Superintendent; and if on such examination he shall be found deficient in the above qualifications, the Society will not make any grant for his travelling expenses or maintenance. It is therefore *particularly requested*, that no person shall be sent to the Seminary, to be trained as a Master, without being provided with the means of defraying his expenses, in case he should not be qualified for admission; nor is he to leave home until written for.

12. The Society has established a regular system for the inspection of all Schools assisted by them, and where the reports of their Inspector are so favourable as to prove that the Master's conduct has been meritorious, the Society gives annual pecuniary gratuities to the Master in proportion to the merit of each case.

13. When Schools are to be conducted on the foregoing principles recommended by the Society, it contributes in proper cases towards the expense of building, furnishing, and fitting up School-houses, and towards providing the Schools with the necessary apparatus of Desks, Forms, Books, Paper, Slates, Slate-pencils and other School Requisites; but in such cases the Society expects that the greater part of the expense shall be borne by the persons residing in the neighbourhood; that a satisfactory assurance shall be given to the Society, that the building shall be permanently used as a School-house; and that the persons applying for aid, shall engage to superintend the School, and to see that the regulations of the Society shall be strictly complied with.

14. The foregoing School Requisites may be procured at the

Depository of the Institution, at *low prices*, for the use of *any School for the instruction of the Poor.*

15. Persons to whom pecuniary grants in aid of building Schools are made, are requested to take notice, that the amount of such grants cannot be paid, until a *particular* account of the *actual expenditure* of the amount granted, specifying *items*, and authenticated by the signatures of two respectable persons residing in the neighbourhood of such Schools, shall have been forwarded to the Committee, together with a Certificate that the shell of the School-house is completed; and when pecuniary aid towards fitting up and furnishing Schools, has been granted, a particular account of the items of the actual expenditure authenticated in like manner, will be required, together with a Certificate that the School is ready and fit for the reception of Scholars, before payment of such grants can be made; and it is necessary that the residences of the individuals signing the Certificates, should be affixed to the documents.

16. With respect to the Books distributed by the Society, it has carefully selected such only as are calculated to convey general instruction and amusement, without imparting or interfering with any *peculiar* religious opinion.

17. When a grant of Books is made to a School, it is not intended that they should be *given* to the Children;—but, that they should become the foundation of a Library attached to the School, and be *lent* to the most deserving Pupils. A cheap mode of rewarding the meritorious is thus provided, and moral and instructive works are more likely to be thus read, when lent, than if they were actually the property of those who borrow them.

18. As the Society cannot, in any instance, do more than *contribute* to the expense of Schools, it is strongly recommended that *local Associations* should be formed for the support of Schools in the neighbourhood of the members of such Associations, and also for the purpose of occasionally inspecting the progress of

the Scholars, *and the conduct of the Masters*: without such superintendence, it is greatly to be feared, there will be many devia-
tions from the system, which ought to be strictly adhered to in
those Schools.

19. It is also recommended, that in all cases the children should
be required to pay a *small* sum weekly. By such means the funds
of the School will be augmented; the poor will set a higher
value on the instruction imparted to them, than they probably
would, if they were entirely indebted to the bounty of others
for their education; and a habit of looking to their own exertions for their support, will be cherished in their minds, which
will prove of essential value to them throughout life.

20. Printed Queries to be answered by persons applying for aid
for Schools, may be procured at the Society's Depository,
Kildare-Place; and it is required that such Queries shall be
answered *on each successive application*, before any grant can be
made for School, or School-master; and no application for aid
can be entertained, that is not respectably authenticated.

21. It is required that all Books and School Requisites purchased from the Society, shall be paid for before they are sent
from the Depository.

22. Books and other articles granted by, or purchased from the
Society, may be left at the Depository until sent for; or they
shall be delivered at any place appointed, *within* the limits of
the City of Dublin.

23. When money is remitted on account of Schools, the Bank
Notes are cut, and one set of halves is kept, until the receipt of
the corresponding halves is acknowledged.

24. If a necessity should occur for changing the name or situation of any School assisted by this Society, such change should
be communicated to the Secretary.

25. It is earnestly requested that when any School assisted by
this Society, has been discontinued, the Secretary be imme-

diately apprized of the circumstance; and that the cause of its discontinuance be stated, together with the means which may be taken to revive it.

26. It is requested that the Managers of Schools assisted by this Society, shall keep accurate registries of the admission, progress, and attendance of the pupils, together with Account Books, containing the particulars of the receipts and expenditure of such Schools.

27. It is also requested that Books shall be kept in the School-room of such Schools, in which Visitors may enter such remarks as to them shall seem fit.

28. The Managers of Schools assisted by this Society, are requested to communicate any information which may be deemed important to such Schools, or to the general objects of the Society; and for this purpose, to keep up a constant and intimate correspondence with the Society, and to be particular in answering the Queries, and, on every application, to give a full account of the School, mentioning any circumstance of importance which shall have occurred subsequent to the preceding applications.

29. In order to render the Cheap Book department of the Institution, as extensively useful as the regulations of the Society permit, it has been determined not to confine the grants of Cheap Books, for Lending Libraries, to Schools in connexion with the Society, but to make grants thereof to all such establishments of a public and charitable nature, as make provision for the preservation of the Books, and for the permanent application of them to the use of the poor. Printed Queries to be answered by applicants for such grants on behalf of such establishments, can be procured at the Society's Depository, Kildare-Place.

30. All letters, Memorials, etc. which are *solely* on the business of this Society, should be directed as follows, in order that they may come free of postage, from any part of Ireland.

Joseph Devonsher Jackson, Esq.
Secretary to the Education Society,
Kildare Place.

And transmitted *unsealed*, under cover, directed

Sir Edward S. Lees,
POST-OFFICE,
Education Society,
Kildare-place   DUBLIN.

Tenth Report of the Society for Promoting the Education of the Poor of Ireland (Dublin, 1822), 58-63

---

17 E. G. Stanley's letter

By 1831, as the Kildare Place Society was no longer acceptable to Catholics, the British government decided to establish a state-subsidised non-sectarian national education system. The constitution of the governing body, the Commissioners of National Education in Ireland, was based on the letter of E. G. Stanley to the Duke of Leinster.

Many English educationists, including Sir James Kay Shuttleworth, visited the Irish schools, and there is little doubt that the formation of the English inspectorate and pupil teacher scheme owes much to this Irish experiment.

LETTER
OF THE
RIGHT HON. E. G. STANLEY,
CHIEF SECRETARY TO HIS EXCELLENCY
THE LORD LIEUTENANT,
ADDRESSED
TO HIS GRACE THE DUKE OF LEINSTER

Irish Office, London, October, 1831.

MY LORD—His Majesty's Government having come to the determination of empowering the Lord Lieutenant to constitute a Board for the superintendence of a system of National Education in Ireland, and Parliament having so far sanctioned the arrangement, as to appropriate a sum of money in the present year, as an experiment of the probable success of the proposed system, I am directed by his Excellency to acquaint your Grace, that it is his intention, with your consent, to constitute you the President of the New Board. And I have it further in command to lay before your Grace the motives of the Government in constituting this Board, the powers which it is intended to confer upon it, and the objects which it is expected that it will bear in view, and carry into effect.

The Commissioners, in 1812, recommended the appointment of a Board of this description, to superintend a system of Education, from which should be banished even the suspicion of proselytism, and which, admitting children of all religious persuasions, should not interfere with the peculiar tenets of any. The Government of the day imagined that they had found a superintending body, acting upon a system such as was recommended, and intrusted the distribution of the National Grants, to the care of the Kildare-street Society. His Majesty's present Government are of opinion, that no private Society, deriving a part, however small, of their annual income from private sources, and only made the channel of the munificence of the Legislature, without being subject to any direct responsibility, could adequately and satisfactorily accomplish the end proposed; and while they do full justice to the liberal views with which that Society was originally instituted, as well as to the fairness with which they have, in most instances, endeavoured to carry their views into effect, they cannot but be sensible that one of the leading principles of that Society was calculated to defeat its avowed objects, as experience has subsequently proved that it has. The determination to enforce in all their Schools the reading of the Holy Scriptures without note or comment, was undoubtedly taken with the purest motives; with the wish at once to connect religious with moral and literary education, and, at the same time, not to run the risk of wounding the peculiar feelings of any sect, by catechetical instruction,

or comments which might tend to subjects of polemical controversy. But it seems to have been overlooked, that the principles
of the Roman Catholic Church (to which, in any system intended for general diffusion throughout Ireland, the bulk of the
pupils must necessarily belong) were totally at variance with
this principle; and that the reading of the Holy Scriptures without note or comment, by children, must be peculiarly obnoxious
to a Church, which denies, even to adults, the right of unaided
private interpretation of the Sacred Volume in articles of
religious belief.

Shortly after its institution, although the Society prospered
and extended its operations under the fostering care of the
Legislature, this vital defect began to be noticed, and the Roman
Catholic Clergy began to exert themselves with energy and
success, against a system to which they were in principle opposed, and which they feared might lead in its results to proselytism, even although no such object were contemplated by
its promoters. When this opposition arose, founded on such
grounds, it soon became manifest that the system could not
become one of National Education.

The Commissioners of Education, in 1824–'25, sensible of the
defects of the system, and of the ground, as well as the strength
of the objection taken, recommended the appointment of two
Teachers in every school, one Protestant, and the other Roman
Catholic, to superintend separately the religious education of
the children: and they hoped to have been able to agree upon a
selection from the Scriptures, which might have been generally
acquiesced in by both persuasions. But it was soon found that
these schemes were impracticable; and in 1828, a Committee of
the House of Commons, to which were referred the various Reports of the Commissioners of Education, recommended a system
to be adopted which should afford, if possible, a combined literary, and a separate religious education, and should be capable
of being so far adapted to the views of the religious persuasions
which divide Ireland, as to render it, in truth, a system of
National Education for the lower classes of the community.

For the success of the undertaking, much must depend upon the character of the individuals who compose the Board; and upon the security thereby afforded to the country, that while the interests of religion are not overlooked, the most scrupulous care should be taken not to interfere with the peculiar tenets of any description of Christian pupils.

To attain the first object, it appears essential that a portion of the Board should be composed of men of high personal character, and of exalted station in the Church; for the latter, that it should consist in part of persons professing different religious opinions.

It is the intention of the Government, that the Board should exercise a complete control over the various schools which may be erected under its auspices, or which, having been already established, may hereafter place themselves under its management, and submit to its regulations. Subject to these, applications for aid will be admissible from Christians of all denominations; but as one of the main objects must be to unite in one system children of different creeds, and as much must depend upon the co-operation of the resident Clergy, the Board will probably look with peculiar favor upon applications proceeding either from,

1st. The Protestant and Roman Catholic Clergy of the Parish; or,
2nd. One of the Clergymen, and a certain number of Parishioners, professing the opposite creed; or,
3rd. Parishioners of both denominations.

Where the application proceeds exclusively from Protestants, or exclusively from Roman Catholics, it will be proper for the Board to make inquiry as to the circumstances which lead to the absence of any names of the persuasion which does not appear.

The Board will note all applications for aid, whether granted or refused, with the grounds of the decision, and annually submit to Parliament a Report of their proceedings.

They will invariably require, as a condition not to be departed from that local funds shall be raised, upon which any aid from the public will be dependent.

They will refuse all applications in which the following objects are not locally provided for:—

1st. A fund sufficient for the annual repairs of the school-house and furniture.

2nd. A permanent salary for the Master, not less than . . . pounds.

3rd. A sum sufficient to purchase books and school requisites at half-price, and books of separate religious instruction at prime cost.

4th. Where aid is required from the Commissioners for building a school-house, it is required that at least one-third of the estimated expense be subscribed, a site for building, to be approved of by the Commissioners, be granted to them, and the school-house, when finished, to be vested in them.

They will require that the Schools be kept open for a certain number of hours, on four or five days of the week, at the discretion of the Commissioners, for moral and literary education only; and that the remaining one or two days in the week be set apart for giving, separately, such religious education to the children, as may be approved of by the Clergy of their respective persuasions.

They will also permit and encourage the Clergy to give religious instruction to the children of their respective persuasions, either before or after the ordinary school hours on the other days of the week.

They will exercise the most entire control over all books to be used in the schools, whether in the combined literary, or separate religious instruction; none to be employed in the first, except under the sanction of the Board, nor in the latter, but with the approbation of the Members of the Board of the persuasion of those for whom they are intended.

They will require that a Register shall be kept in the Schools, in which shall be entered the attendance or non-attendance of each child on Divine Worship on Sundays.

They will, at various times, either by themselves, or by their Inspectors, visit and examine into the state of each School, and report their observations to the Board.

They will allow to the individuals or bodies applying for aid, the appointment of their own Teacher, subject to the following restrictions and Regulations:

1st. He (or she) shall be liable to be fined, suspended, or removed altogether, by the authority of the Commissioners, who shall, however, record their reasons.

2nd. He shall have received previous instruction in a Model School, to be established in Dublin,

N.B.—It is not intended that this regulation should apply to prevent the admission of masters or mistresses of schools already established, who may be approved of by the Commissioners, nor of such as the Board may think fit to appoint, before the proposed Model School may come into full operation.

3rd. He shall have received testimonials of good conduct and of general fitness for the situation, from the Board, or the persons employed by them to conduct the Model School.

The Board will be intrusted with the absolute control over the funds which may be annually voted by Parliament, which they shall apply to the following purposes:—

1st. Granting aid for the erection of schools, subject to the conditions hereinbefore specified.

2nd. Paying Inspectors for visiting and reporting upon schools.

3rd. Gratuities to Teachers of schools conducted under the Rules laid down, not exceeding . . . Pounds each.

4th. Establishing and maintaining a Model School in Dublin, and training Teachers for country schools.

5th. Editing and printing such books of moral and literary

education as may be approved of for the use of the schools,
and supplying them and school necessaries, at not lower
than half-price.

I have thus stated the objects which His Majesty's Government have in view, and the principal regulations by which they
think those objects may be most effectually promoted; and I
am directed by the Lord Lieutenant to express His Excellency's
earnest wish that the one and the other may be found such as to
procure for the Board the sanction of your Grace's name, and
the benefit of your Grace's attendance.

A full power will, of course, be given to the Board to make
such regulations upon matters of detail, not inconsistent with
the spirit of these Instructions, as they may judge best qualified
to carry into effect the intentions of the Government and of the
Legislature. Parliament has already placed at his Excellency's
disposal a sum which may be available even in the course of the
present year; and as soon as the Board can be formed, it will be
highly desirable that no time should be lost, with a view to the
estimates of the ensuing year, in enabling such schools, already
established, as are willing to subscribe to the conditions imposed, to put in their claims for protection and assistance; and
in receiving applications from parties desirous to avail themselves of the munificence of the Legislature, in founding new
schools under your regulations.

I have the honor to be, my Lord,

Your Grace's most obedient Servant,

E. G. STANLEY.

To His Grace the Duke of Leinster,

etc. etc.

First Report of the Commissioners of National Education in Ireland
(1834)

18 Quarterly Journal of Education   Towards secular education

After the disturbances of 1830 the Society for the Diffusion of

Useful Knowledge accused the religious societies of having failed to provide a relevant schooling for their pupils. The Society criticised the usefulness of a scriptural education and argued that it would be better to have state schools educating children for the machine age. The *Quarterly Journal of Education* was established in 1831 to campaign for secular state education.

REASONS FOR ESTABLISHING A PUBLIC SYSTEM OF ELEMENTARY INSTRUCTION IN ENGLAND

In our last number we gave some account of the institutions that have been established in Scotland, the United States, Prussia, Hesse, Bavaria, etc., for affording elementary instruction to the lower classes; and endeavoured, at the same time, briefly to point out the advantages that had resulted from the consequent diffusion of education in these countries. But we take leave to say, that elementary instruction is no where so indispensable as in England and Ireland; and yet they are now among the few civilized countries in which no public provision has been made for its supply. Not only are the means of education very deficient amongst us, but the quality of that which is afforded by the benevolent efforts of individuals is, and must unavoidably continue to be, very defective. This is much to be lamented: the state of society in England is, in many respects, peculiar, or rather, we should say, without a parallel either in ancient or modern times. Owing to the extraordinary extension of manufactures and commerce amongst us, and to the mode in which landed property is occupied, a very large proportion of our people is dependent for support on the wages of labour, and is consequently exposed to all the vicissitudes that necessarily result from so precarious a condition. Changes of policy or fashion, abroad or at home, may, at any time, deprive thousands upon thousands of our labouring population of their accustomed means of subsistence; while any serious deficiency in the harvest is sure to inflict the severest privations on the whole class. The situation of the labourers of all other countries is widely different; manufactures and commerce have made comparatively little progress amongst them; the greater number of their inhabitants are attached to the soil and depend upon it for support, so that the proportion of those liable to be thrown out of employment is comparatively small.

This peculiar state of things ought to excite the deep and earnest attention of those interested in the welfare of the country. It would be easy to show that it has many advantages, and in particular, that it is highly favourable to the progress of the arts, and gives the fullest scope to invention: but, on the other hand, it is pregnant with no inconsiderable amount of danger. The labourers are now become, from their number and their union, in the large manufacturing towns, one of the most important powers in the state, and exercise a very great influence over the deliberations and acts of government. No one who has any, even the slightest, practical acquaintance with the workings of our political system can doubt the truth of this statement; and as little can it be doubted that this power is becoming every day more formidable. Need we say more to prove that it is of the utmost importance, not only as respects the stability of our institutions, and the security of the middle and upper classes, but as respects all the best interests of the labourers themselves, that every possible effort should be made to diffuse *sound instruction*. Education may be dispensed with in other countries, but it cannot be dispensed with in England. It is not to be denied that a manufacturing population is peculiarly inflammable, and apt to be misled; and the only way to secure the labourers, as well as the other classes, from the ruinous consequences that are sure to arise from their supporting any unsound or impracticable principle, is to instruct them in their real interests.

The poor are neither fools nor knaves; they investigate all plain practical questions with quite as much sagacity and penetration as those that are rich: and were they made aware of the circumstances which really determine their condition, they would, speaking generally, be disinclined to do anything that might tend to render it worse. To suppose that it should be otherwise would be to suppose what is contradictory and absurd; it would be to suppose that they are insensible to, and careless of, their own interest! Is it not, then, the duty of all governments, but especially of the government of a country so peculiarly situated as England, to make provision for the proper education of the poor? If any one ask what has elevated the British empire to the high pitch of wealth and power she has attained, the answer is obvious, and may be made in two words —*freedom* and *security*: Freedom to engage in any sort of undertaking, and to prosecute it in one's own way, combined with the conviction, or sense of security, felt by every one, that he will be allowed to employ or dispose of his property without molestation. Without security there can be neither riches nor civilization; and, however far a country may have advanced, if she do not, at all hazards, maintain the security of property, she will speedily relapse into primeval barbarism and ignorance. But what is, of all others, the most effectual means of providing for this security? Will it be best promoted by multiplying penal statutes? by maintaining large bodies of military and police? or by making one half the population responsible for the other? We confidently answer, No: not that we mean to say or to insinuate that punishments, troops, police, etc. are not indispensable; but they are not enough. The foundations of real security are beyond and above the law. Outrage and attack may and ought to be put down by prompt and adequate punishment; but no severity of punishment, provided the circumstances in which the outrages originated be not changed, will hinder them from breaking out anew. And hence, if we would have perfect security, as perfect at least as can be obtained, we must show the people that it is for their advantage that it should be preserved inviolate; we must prove to them—and luckily the proof is very easy—that whatever has any tendency to shake the security of property, is even more ruinous to those who depend upon wages for subsistence than to their employers. Make a labourer aware that the introduction of machinery is highly

beneficial to his order—that, in fact, it has more than quin-
tupled the demand for labour, and added prodigiously to the
comforts and conveniences of every class—and, though he were
the veriest clodpole that ever existed, machinery will cease to be
the object of his attack. Men often traduce and calumniate their
benefactors; but they invariably do so in ignorance, and because they believe them to be their enemies; undeceive them
upon this point, and their ingratitude is immediately changed
into gratitude and esteem;—so it is with attacks on property.
The Luddites and the peasantry believe that machinery is hostile to them, that it deprives them of employment, and drives
them to the workhouse, and they, therefore, destroy it; nor can
anything, under such circumstances, be more natural. The law,
indeed, says that machinery shall be protected, and that those
who attempt its demolition shall be punished; and no reasonable man can dispute the expediency of such a regulation. But
it is obvious, as well from the nature of the thing as from what
has taken place amongst us, that the threatenings of the law are
not sufficient for the prevention of outrage; and seeing, as every
one does, that such is the case, is it not incumbent upon us to
try what may be done by other means? It is all very proper to
tell the labourers that they shall be sent to the gibbet or the
hulks if they commit certain acts; but would it not give weight
to such tremendous denunciations, were means at the same
time adopted for proving, to the conviction of the labourers,
that the law is not hostile to them; that the acts it denounces are
as destructive of their interests as of those of others; and that the
security of property and the employment and continued improvement of machinery are, in fact, indispensable to the
existence of the great bulk of the labouring class? Satisfy the
labourers that such is the case, and there will be no more occasion for special commissions. Not one in ten thousand can
honestly exclaim *video meliora proboque, detiora sequor*! We are
inimical to whatever we believe to be injurious to ourselves, and
though the laws of Draco were enacted over again, we should
take the first opportunity of displaying our enmity by some overt

act. The lash, and nothing else, is powerful enough to compel the slave to sluggish exertion; but the desire to promote his own advantage is sufficient to make the freeman laborious and inventive. In like manner, penal statutes may make those who are ignorant, and who are probably misled by designing knaves, unwillingly respect, for a while, the right of property; whereas an instructed population willingly respect it for their own sakes, and because they know it is essential to their welfare.

We have referred to the case of machinery, because of the open and multiplied attacks that have been made upon it; but they are very ignorant indeed of what is going on around them who suppose that hostility to machinery is the only or the most dangerous delusion that is growing up amongst the labouring classes. And let no one imagine that so mighty a power can be dragooned or coerced into obedience—No! if we would make sure of the permanent tranquillity, and by consequence of the permanent prosperity of the empire, we must address ourselves to the reason and not to the fears of the multitude; we must show them wherein their real interest lies; and to do this we must supply them with that of which they are now entirely destitute—a really good and useful system of instruction. We must give to the poor the means of distinguishing between their apparent and their real interests, and of detecting the pernicious sophistry of those who make it their business to delude them. Hitherto it would seem as if those who have promoted the education of the poor imagined they had done quite enough when they taught them to read and write. But though this much be indispensable, still it is certain that the education which stops at this point is most incomplete, and may, indeed, be perverted to the very worst purposes. A knowledge of the arts of reading, writing, and arithmetic may, and frequently does, exist along with the most profound ignorance of all those things as to which it is most essential that the poor should be informed; it opens an inlet to truth, but so does it to error and sophistry; and it is the bounden duty of the rulers of every country, at least if they would make sure of their own safety,

F

and provide for the welfare of their people, to take especial care, not only that the avenues to knowledge shall be opened to the poor, but that they shall be instructed in the mode of distinguishing what is true from what is false—at least in so far as their leading interests and those of society are involved. For this reason we look upon it as indispensable, that besides being instructed in the arts of reading and writing, provision should be made for instructing the labouring classes in those circumstances which have the greatest influence over their condition. They should, first of all, be made acquainted with the motives which have induced every society emerging from barbarism to establish the right of property; and the advantages resulting from its establishment, and the necessity of maintaining it inviolate, should be clearly set forth. The sophisms of those who contend that property is instituted only for the advantage of the rich should be exposed; for though it cannot be shown that the institution of private property has made all men rich, it may very easily be shown that it has done ten times more than all other institutions put together to produce that effect; and that were it subverted, the rich man would very soon become poor, while he that is at present poor would become still poorer. The circumstances that give rise to those gradations of rank and fortune that actually exist ought also to be explained: it may be shown that they are as natural to society as differences of sex, of strength, or of colour; and that though such a revolution were to take place as should overthrow all that is exalted, and establish the Spencean system on the ruins of the present order of things, the equality thus violently and unjustly brought about could not be maintained for a week; and that infinite misery would be inflicted on society without obtaining any countervailing good whatever.

The next object should be to make the poor fully acquainted with the various benefits resulting from the employment of machinery in industrious undertakings; and they should be shown, that though such employment may sometimes appear to lessen the demand for labour, its real effect is *always to increase it*; and that their interests are invariably promoted by the adoption of every device that can in any way add to the powers of production.

But it is, above all, necessary that the labourers, and indeed that every class, should be acquainted with the circumstances that determine the rate of wages, or with the plain and elementary principles respecting population and the demand for labour. . . . *Quarterly Journal of Education*, Vol I (1831), 213–18

19 Richard Whateley   Easy Lessons on Money Matters

The Society for the Diffusion of Useful Knowledge was anxious to introduce political economy into the school curriculum to help the working classes to learn their role in an industrial society. In 1833 Richard Whateley, Archbishop of Dublin and also one of the Irish Commissioners of National Education, published a booklet called *Easy Lessons on Money Matters*. Extracts from *Easy Lessons* were read by several generations of schoolchildren in Britain and her colonies. The extract that follows was reproduced in almost every set of readers published between 1834 and 1880.

RICH AND POOR

BESIDES those who work for their living, some at a higher rate and some at a lower, there are others who do not live by their labour at all, but are rich enough to subsist on what they or their fathers have laid up. There are many of these rich men, indeed, who do hold laborious offices, as magistrates and members of parliament. But this is at their own choice. They do not labour for their subsistence, but live on their property.

There can be but few of such persons, compared with those who are obliged to work for their living, but though there can be no country where all, or the greater part, are rich enough to live without labour, there are several countries where all are poor; and in those countries where all are forced to live by their labour, the people are much worse off than most of the labourers are in this country. In savage nations almost every one is half starved at times, and generally half naked. But in any country in which property is secure, and the people industrious, the wealth of that country will increase; and those who are the most industrious and frugal will gain more than such as are idle and extravagant, and will lay by something for their children, who will thus be born to a good property.

Young people who make good use of their time, are quick at learning, and grow up industrious and steady, may, perhaps, be able to earn more than enough for their support, and so have the satisfaction of leaving some property to their children; and if they, again, should, instead of spending this property, increase it by honest diligence, prudence, and frugality, they may, in time, raise themselves to wealth. Several of the richest families in the country have risen in this manner from a low station. It is, of course, not to be expected that *many* poor men should become rich, nor ought any man to set his heart on being so; but it is an allowable and a cheering thought, that no one is shut out from the hope of bettering his condition, and providing for his children.

And would you not think it hard that a man should not be allowed to lay by his savings for his children? But this is the case in some countries, where property is so ill secured that a man is liable to have all his savings forced from him, or seized upon at his death; and there all the people are miserably poor, because no one thinks it worth his while to attempt saving anything.

There are some countries which were formerly very productive and populous, but which now, under the tyrannical government of the Turks, or other such people, have become almost deserts. In former times Barbary produced silk, but now most of the mulberry-trees (on whose leaves the silk-worms are fed) are decayed ; and no one thinks of planting fresh trees, because he has no security that he shall be allowed to enjoy the produce.

Can it be supposed that the poor would be better off if all the property of the rich were taken away and divided among them,

and no one allowed to become rich for the future? The poor
would then be much worse off than they are now; they would
still have to work for their living as they do now, for food and
clothes cannot be had without *somebody's* labour. But they
would not work near so profitably as they do now, because no
one would be able to keep up a large manufactory or farm well
stocked, and to advance wages to workmen, as is done now, for
work which does not bring in any return for, perhaps, a year or
two. Every man would live, as the saying is, "from hand to
mouth," just tilling his own little patch of ground, enough to
keep him alive, and not daring to lay by anything, because if he
were supposed to be rich, he would be in danger of having his
property taken away and divided.

And if a bad crop, or a sickly family, brought any one into
distress, which would soon be the case with many, what would
he do after he had spent his little property? He would be willing
to work for hire, but no one could afford to employ him, except
in something that would bring in a very speedy return; for even
those few who might have saved a little money would be afraid
to have it known, for fear of being forced to part with it. They
would hide it somewhere in a hole in the ground, which used
formerly to be a common practice in this country, and still is in
some others, where property is very scarce. Under such a state
of things the whole country would become poorer and poorer
every year: for each man would labour no more than just
enough for his immediate supply, and would also employ his
labour less profitably than now, for want of a proper division of
labour; and no one would attempt to lay by anything, because
he would not be sure of being allowed to keep it. In consequence
of all this, the whole produce of the land and the labour of the
country would become much less than it is now; and we should
soon be reduced to the same general wretchedness and distress
which prevails in many half-savage countries. The rich, indeed,
would have become poor; but the poor, instead of improving
their condition, would be much worse off than before. All
would soon be as miserably poor as the most destitute beggars

are now: indeed, so far worse, that *there would be nobody to beg of.*

It is best for all parties, the rich, the poor, the middling, that property should be secure, and that every one should be allowed to possess what is his own, to gain whatever he can by honest means, and keep it or spend it as he thinks fit;—provided he does no one any injury. Some rich men, indeed, make a much better use of their fortunes than others: but one who is ever so selfish in his disposition can hardly help spending it on his neighbours. If a man has an income of £5,000 a year, some people might think, at first sight, that if his estate were divided among one hundred poor families, which would give each of them £50 a-year, there would thus be, by such a division, one hundred poor families the more enabled to subsist in the country. But this is quite a mistake. Such would, indeed, be the case, if the rich man had been used to eat as much food as one hundred poor families, and to wear out as much clothes as all of them. But we know this is not the case. He pays away his income to servants, and labourers, and tradesmen, and manufacturers of different articles, who lay out the money in food and clothing for their families: so that in reality the same sort of division of it is made as if it had been taken away from him. He may, perhaps, if he be a selfish man, care nothing for the maintaining of all these families, but still he does maintain them; for if he should choose to spend £1,000 a-year in fine pictures, the painters who are employed in those pictures are as well maintained as if he had made them a present of the money, and left them to sit idle. The only difference is, that they feel they are honestly earning their living, instead of subsisting on charity; but the total quantity of food and clothing in the country is neither the greater nor the less in the one case than in the other. But if a rich man, instead of spending all his income, saves a great part of it, this saving will almost always be the means of maintaining a still greater number of industrious people: for a man who saves, hardly ever, in these days at least, hoards up gold and silver in a box, but lends it out on good security, that he may receive interest upon it. Suppose, instead of spending £1,000 a-year on paintings, he saves that sum every year. Then this money is generally borrowed by farmers, or manufacturers, or merchants, who can make a profit by it in the way of their business, over and above the interest they pay for the use of it. And in order to do this, they lay it out in employing labourers to till the ground, or to manufacture cloth and other articles, or to import foreign goods: by which means the corn, and cloth, and other commodities of the country, are increased.

The rich man, therefore, though he appears to have so much larger a share allotted to him, does not really consume it, but is only the channel through which it flows to others. And it is by this means much better distributed than it could have been otherwise.

The mistake of which I have been speaking, of supposing that the rich cause the poor to be worse off, was exposed long ago in the fable of the stomach and the limbs:—

"Once on a time," says the fable, "all the other members of the body began to murmur against the stomach, for employing the labours of all the rest, and consuming all they had helped to provide, without doing anything in return. So they all agreed to strike work, and refused to wait upon this idle stomach any longer. The feet refused to carry it about; the hands resolved to put no food into the mouth for it; the nose refused to smell for it, and the eyes to look out in its service; and the ears declared they would not even listen to the dinner-bell; and so of all the rest. But after the stomach had been left empty for some time, all the members began to suffer. The legs and arms grew feeble; the eyes became dim, and all the body languid and exhausted.

" 'Oh, foolish members,' said the stomach, 'you now perceive that what you used to supply to me, was in reality supplied to yourselves. I did not consume for myself the food that was put into me, but digested it, and prepared it for being changed into blood, which was sent through various channels as a supply for each of you. If you are occupied in feeding me, it is by me in turn, that the blood-vessels which nourish you are fed.' "

You see then, that a rich man, even though he may care for no one but himself, can hardly avoid benefiting his neighbours. But this is no merit of his, if he himself has no desire or wish to benefit them. On the other hand, a rich man who seeks for deserving objects to relieve and assist, and is, as the apostle expresses, "ready to give, and glad to distribute, is laying up in store for himself a good foundation for the time to come, that he may lay hold of eternal life." It is plain from this, and from many other such injunctions of the apostles, that they did not intend to destroy the security of property among Christians, which leads to the distinction between the rich and the poor; for their exhortations to the rich to be kind and charitable to the poor, would have been absurd if they had not allowed that any of their people should be rich; and there could be no such thing as charity in giving anything to the poor, if it were not left to each man's free choice to give or spend what is his own. Indeed, nothing can be called your own which you are not left free to dispose of as you will. The very nature of charity implies that it must be voluntary: for no one can be properly said to *give* anything that he has no power to withhold. The Apostle Paul, indeed, goes yet farther, when he desires each man "to *give* according as he is disposed in his heart, and not grudgingly," because "God loveth the cheerful giver."

When men are thus left to their own inclinations to make use of their money, each as he is disposed in his heart, we must expect to find that some will choose to spend it merely on their own selfish enjoyments. Such men, although, as you have seen, they do contribute to maintain many industrious families without intending it, yet are themselves not the less selfish and odious. But still we are not the less forbidden to rob, or defraud, or annoy them. Scripture forbids us to "covet our neighbour's goods," not because he does not make a right use of them, but because they are *his*.

When you see a rich man who is proud and selfish, perhaps

you are tempted to think how much better a use you would make of wealth if you were as rich as he. I hope you would: but the best *proof* that you can give that you would behave well if you were in *another's* place, is by behaving well *in your own*. God has appointed to each his own trials, and his own duties; and He will judge you, not according to what you think you would have done in some different station, but according to what you *have* done in that station in which he has placed you. Commissioners of National Education in Ireland, *Fourth Book of Lessons* (1850)

---

20 James Simpson   Elijah and the goats

Many educationists had doubts about scriptural education and an increasing number publicly condemned it. Perhaps the most devastating attack came from James Simpson, a Scottish educationist.

. . . Would you exclude altogether from the elementary school religious teaching as based upon Christianity?—Not from the *school*, but with regard to the *secular teacher*; I would secularize secular education wholly, and not partially.

Would you prohibit the teacher from any reference, in the course of his lessons, to Christian doctrines or Christian history, as such?—It would be better to do so.

How would you make provision for the teaching of the Christian religion?—I would, as I have said, secularize secular education wholly, as such, but at the same time make a most perfect provision for education in revealed religion, and this I should do by allotting to every elementary school both secular and religious instruction, but under different teachers and at separate hours. And my reasons for doing so are these: first, secular and religious truth, though from the same God, are distinct in their sources and evidence. I hold it to be unphilosophical to blend them, and confound in the young mind the difference of their source and evidence, because each gains strength from the fact of arising separately, yet meeting in one centre of truth. The benefit of this strong, because double foundation for religion, is lost where revealed religion is appealed to authoritatively, as controlling philosophical or secular truth. This is the opinion of eminent divines and Christian moralists. Melancthon recognises this distinct origin when he says, "Wherefore our decision is this, that these precepts, which learned men have committed to writing, transcribing them from the common reason and common feelings of human nature, are to be accounted as not less divine than those contained in the tables given to Moses; and that it could not be the intention of our Maker to supersede, by a law graven upon stone, that which is written with his own finger on the table of the heart." This view of Melancthon's is confirmed by Cudworth, Adam Smith, Reid, Dugald Stewart and Thomas Brown, and, I may add, Paley. These philosophers all lay down or assume the same important doctrine. To confound secular and religious knowledge is to injure both. First, secular knowledge is thus injured; it is apt to be limited and controlled, not so much by Scripture, as by the particular interpretations that different sects choose to put upon Scripture, that is, in 70 or 80 different ways, which is about the number of well-distinguished sects in this country, till its own origin in eternal truth is broken down, obscured, and lost. Assuming that all sound philosophy and all true religion must harmonize, there is a manifest advantage in cultivating *each by itself*; till its full dimensions, limits and applications shall be brought clearly to light. We may *then* advantageously compare them, and use the one as a means of elucidating our views of the other.

Have you any examples in support of your statement?—I know schools, with well-meaning but imperfectly-educated directors, where the Bible is the school-book, the only school-book; where a large Bible is selected and placed upon a stand in the middle of the school, impressing, at least leaving the impression to take effect, upon the minds of the young, that the Bible is the only book in the world, and addressing to it something almost of an idolatrous respect. In those schools every lesson, however secular, arises out of, and comes back to the Bible: for example, if the lesson should be the natural history of the bear, it will not be permitted to be entered into till the passage is read about the bears that tore the children that mocked Elijah; and if the lesson should peradventure turn to the goat, the description of the day of judgment, with the goats upon the left hand and the sheep upon the right, is first found out and read. This leads to the inculcation of the hurtful error (for I hold that by the arrangements of the Creator no error is harmless) that the Bible is given to teach all knowledge, scientific included, and that nothing can be true which is not to be found there. The question in such schools always is, what does the Bible say upon this point? and the error is inculcated that God has opened only one, and not two great books, the book of Nature as well as the book of Revelation, and has not made the one to throw light upon the other, provided they are separately studied. The effect of this upon secular knowledge is such as to unfit young people so trained for after-life; the mind is weakened and injured by it, and it will be practically found that the children coming from such schools will be exceedingly imperfectly educated, if they can be said to be educated at all. In those of them who have particularly excitable temperaments, religious feelings will take hold often to a dangerous extent, so as to subject the young person to the influences of fanaticism and (if there is a predisposition) to religious insanity. But in the great majority of cases it will operate in the way of disgust, by over-doing religious instruction, and the Bible and the reiterated instructions will be all thrown away whenever the pupil escapes into freedom. It is in this way I hold, secondly, that religion is injured by this mode of education, and the end is defeated, for over-doing is always attended with disgust. It happens, in striking confirmation, that a report given in to the General Assembly of the Church of Scotland, by their committee of superintendence of education in the Highland Schools, particularly dwells upon the fact, that the visitors always found the pupils who had made most progress in secular knowledge the best instructed in religious. I should hold also that the tendency to over-do and over-task by religious instruction in infant schools, is perhaps one of the most effectual ways of abusing those institutions, in the way cautioned against by Dr. Brigham, that can be conceived. There is so great a zeal and anxiety on the part of the religious to inculcate religion, that they think they never can over-do it, and therefore the infant brain is over-worked by an excess of religious instruction, and runs the risk of being injured by that which ought to be made, if properly inculcated, a source of pleasure, being made a source of unsuitable intellectual labour. . . . *Select Committee on Education in England and Wales*, 185–6, PP, 1835 (465), VII

___

21 British and Foreign School Society The Daily Lesson Book (1839)
In 1839 the British and Foreign School Society gave way to its critics and published its first secular reader, to be a companion text to *Scripture Lessons*. Below is an extract from the preface and one of the lessons.

___

PREFACE
THE main DESIGN of the present volume, which will ultimately be preceded by others of a more elementary character, and will then form the third of a Series of Reading Books, is to favour the production of good moral and religious influences in connexion with a rigorous course of intellectual instruction and discipline. With this view each day's lesson has been made to include, first, a text of Holy Scripture, which, being committed to memory, may serve as a motto for the day; secondly, a brief poetical extract, adapted to improve the taste and excite the affections; and, lastly, a portion of useful knowledge intended as a general exercise in reading. To each of these portions, Analyses and practical lessons have been appended, in the form of notes, at the foot of every page.

The CLASS OF CHILDREN for whom the book is specially intended, are supposed to have overcome to a considerable extent the mechanical difficulty of reading, and to be already prepared, with a little assistance, not only to comprehend the general scope and bearing of a writer, but in some degree to appreciate the value or beauty of his thoughts. It is precisely at this period,—just when the pupil is *beginning to enjoy* the perusal of a book, that the present volume should be introduced.

The following may be regarded as its DISTINCTIVE FEATURES:—

1. In the space of two pages *an adequate and varied portion* is provided for each day's instruction, every lesson being complete in itself—the notes furnishing a clue to all needful explanations.

2. The PIECES SELECTED are of a kind directly calculated to improve the mind and character of the reader. The Poetry will be found to favour loving and trustful feelings,—a taste for the enjoyment of natural scenery,—and the cultivation of a humble, contented, and domestic spirit. The prose pieces include extracts relating to natural history, travels, home and foreign productions, the elements of political economy, slavery, war, temperance, economy, cleanliness, trust-worthiness, obedience to laws, sanctification of the Sabbath, piety, etc. etc.

3. The ANALYSES are prepared on a new plan, including not merely the roots of words, but everything requisite to the most exact understanding of the lesson, as well as to the practical application of it, both to the intellect and to the heart.*

4. The SATURDAY'S LESSON proceeds on the assumption that a part of this day is generally devoted in good schools to recapitulatory exercises. It is therefore half the usual length, and consists simply of illustrations of words or things which have been referred to in the course of the week, and which

---

* The editors are perfectly aware that the information given in the notes will be superfluous to many teachers; but though not *needed* by such, it may occasionally be *convenient* even to them to have at hand the precise information required to illustrate a lesson. To junior assistants such aids are indispensable. . . .

could not be fully explained in the small space devoted to analytical notes.

5. The SIMULTANEOUS LESSON, of which a brief outline only is furnished, should be given orally by the teacher to the children when seated at their desks or in a gallery. It should take the character of a familiar and colloquial lecture; and in order to secure attention, it should be broken in upon by brief questions, and enlivened by the introduction of elliptical sentences,—the children being called upon to fill up the pause by supplying an appropriate word. In this way the interest of a class or of the whole school may be sustained for at least twenty minutes, beyond which time it is not advisable to lengthen the address. At the close, those who can write with sufficient facility should be directed to put down from memory what they can recollect of the lecture. This exercise will be found eminently useful, not only in forming habits of attention, but also in facilitating the expression of thought with ease and accuracy.

THE EDITORS

DAILY READING LESSON—WEDNESDAY

TEXT FOR THE DAY.—Prov. xvi. 1.—"*The preparations of the heart in man, and the answer of the tongue, is from the Lord.*"

HEALTH

"I care not, Fortune, what you me deny;
　　You cannot rob me of free Nature's grace,
　You cannot shut the windows of the sky,
　　Through which Aurora shows her brightening face;
　　You cannot bar my constant feet to trace
　The woods and lawns by living stream at eve;
　　Let health my nerves and finer fibres brace,

And I their toys to the *rich children* leave;
Of fancy, reason, virtue, nought can me bereave."*

Thomson

HEALTH—CLEANLINESS

"When we consider how large a portion of the Divine moral law relates to our duty to our neighbours, and how much filthy habits are injurious to them, as well as to those who adopt them, we surely need feel no hesitation in admitting the truth of the remark, that cleanliness is next to godliness.

You are probably aware that the plague, in its most fearful forms, used formerly to visit, with almost exterminating severity, many cities in which it has long since been wholly unknown. London affords one of the most striking examples which I could adduce. . . . Henry Dunn and John Thomas Crossley. *Daily Lesson Book No. III* (1839)

---

22 A day at Borough Road School

In the 1830s the monitorial system was still widely employed. The teacher training manual, from which the following passages are taken, shows how children spent their day at the British and Foreign School Society's Borough Road School.

FIRST CLASS—THE ALPHABET

IN this class there were no boys, the alphabet not being taught in the usual way,—a single letter at a time, but in connexion with words having a definite meaning; a plan which

* SUBJECT. *The pleasures of fancy, reason, virtue, far greater than those which riches yield.*
ANALYSIS. *Fortune,* fig. pers. sen. money and its advantages. *free,* sen. open to all. *grace,* sen. beauties. *windows,* fig. meta. sen. through which light passes. *Aurora,* sen. day, or its cause, the sun. *bar.* i.e. stop. *living,* sen. as ever moving, or being full of living things. *nerves,* i.e. small sensitive threads. *toys,* splendid things, coaches, horses, etc. *children,* all persons being amused with trifles. *reason,* sen. reflective power. *virtue,* sen. goodness.
LESSON. Riches are only one gift among the many gifts of God, and there are many gifts more valuable than that of riches.

experience has found to be the best. The second class likewise contained no boys, they having been removed into the third, or words of three letters.

THIRD CLASS—WORDS OF THREE LETTERS

Monitor. Spell BEE. B e e.—What is a bee? A little insect. —What is it fond of? One boy: Sugar. Another boy: Flowers. We asked what sort of flowers? One boy: I know, only I forgot; boys afterwards said, roses, tulips, butter-cups.—What else is a bee fond of, what does it like to do? Work.—How does the bee work? Gathers honey. One little boy repeated, "How doth the little busy bee."—Who ought to work? Every body.—What for? To get their living.—What ought not those to do who are lazy? They ought not to eat.—When do boys work? When they go of errands for their mothers; when they come to school.

CUP. Questioned by the Monitor. What is a cup made of? Gold, silver, china.—Who drinks out of gold cups? The king.— Who drinks out of china cups? The gentlepeople.—Who drinks out of earthenware cups? Poor people.—What is drunk out of cups? Tea, coffee.—Where does tea come from?—Where does coffee come from?—What is the inside of a cup? Hollow.—The outside? Convex.—What is the edge called? The brim.

FOURTH CLASS—WORDS OF FOUR LETTERS

MIND. Spell mind. What is mind? The thinking part of man.—What is the most important subject we can think about? Religion.—What is religion? Thinking about God and doing his will.—What do you think you ought to do? Pray to him, praise him, keep his word.—What do you mean by keeping his word? Obey what he says.—Where do you find what God says? In the Bible.—What is said there that we ought to do? To love God, to fear him. Another boy: To love our parents, to love one another.—Ought you to hate any thing? Yes, sin.—What is sin? Breaking of God's law. Another: Wickedness—How could you sin against your father and mother? By not doing what they bid us, not to love them.—Tell me something you might do in school that would be sin. To strike a boy, not mind our monitor. —If a boy was to strike you, what ought you to do? Forgive him.—How often? Always.—Who was struck and would not strike again? Jesus Christ.—Who struck him? The soldiers.— What did Jesus say when he was ill-used? Father, forgive them: they know not what they do.—What part of the Lord's Prayer speaks of forgiveness? Forgive us our trespasses.

CORN. What is corn? Different kinds of grain.—Name some. Wheat, rye, oats, barley.—What do you make from wheat? Flour.—What of flour? Bread.—How is the flour made? The wheat is ground in a mill.—What turns the mill? Wind, water, horses, steam.—What is made of barley? Malt, beer.—Tell me some kinds of beer. Ale, porter, table beer.— What is the use of oats? To make oatmeal, and to feed horses, fowls, and rabbits.—What do you make of oatmeal? Gruel.

FIFTH CLASS

(*In this class the boys commence reading easy portions of Scripture.*)
BOY READS—"For this God is our God for ever and ever; he will be our guide even unto death."

What God is this? Our God.—Is he any other people's God? Yes, those that believe in him.—What are those people called who do not believe in him? Atheists.—What do some people make to worship as a god? Images. What are these people called? Idolators, Heathens.—In what parts of the world are people heathen? In China, in Hindoostan.—What are those people called who go to preach the true God? Missionaries.— What did the Jews call God? Jehovah.—What sort of a being is God? He is holy. Another boy: He is wise. Another: He is good, he is omnipotent. What is that? Able to do every thing. How long is he our God? For ever and ever.—What has he given for our guide in his will. One boy: The Bible. Another: The commandments. Another: Sent Jesus Christ. Another: Ministers to preach. Another: A Church.—What else to act on our minds? The Spirit of truth; Christ, "the true light, that lighteth every man that cometh into the world." Another: The

G

Holy Spirit. Another: The Holy Ghost.—What for? To guide
us, to comfort us, to show us we are sinners.

(*This class spells words of two syllables.*)
SACRED. What is sacred? Holy.—Tell me something sacred!
The Bible, the Holy Scriptures, the New Testament. Another
boy: The name of God.—Prove that from Scripture? "Holy
and reverend is his name;" . . . Henry Dunn. *Principles of
Teaching* (9th ed, c 1850; 1st ed, 1837), 252–5

23 Statistical Society investigations

Despite all the efforts of the religious societies much remained to be done. In the 1830s the statistical societies in-
vestigated educational facilities in a number of towns. This
report, dealing with Manchester, is typical.

The Committee beg to call the attention of the Society to
the following remarks on each different class of Schools that
have been visited during the enquiry:—

DAME SCHOOLS

Under this head are included all those schools in which reading only, and a little sewing, are taught. This is the most
numerous class of schools, and they are generally in the most
deplorable condition. The greater part of them are kept by
females, but some by old men, whose only qualification for this
employment seems to be their unfitness for every other. Many
of these teachers are engaged at the same time in some other
employment, such as shopkeeping, sewing, washing, etc. which
renders any regular instruction among their scholars absolutely
impossible. Indeed, neither parents nor teachers seem to consider this as the principal object, in sending the children to
these schools, but generally say that they go there in order to be
taken care of, and to be out of the way at home.*

* Yet it is curious that a very frequent objection made against Infant
Schools both by the parents and teachers, was, that the children *learn no-*

These schools are generally found in very dirty unwholesome rooms—frequently in close damp cellars, or old dilapidated garrets. In one of these schools eleven children were found, in a small room, in which one of the children of the Mistress was lying in bed ill of the measles. Another child had died in the same room, of the same complaint a few days before; and no less than thirty of the usual scholars were then confined at home with the same disease.

In another school all the children to the number of twenty, were squatted upon the bare floor there being no benches, chairs, or furniture of any kind, in the room. The Master said his terms would not yet allow him to provide forms, but he hoped that as his school increased, and his circumstances thereby improved, he should be able sometime or other to afford this luxury.

In by far the greater number of these schools there were only two or three books among the whole number of scholars. In others there was not one; and the children depended for their instruction on the chance of some one of them bringing a book, or a part of one from home. Books however, are occasionally provided by the Mistress, and in this case the supply is somewhat greater; but in almost all cases, it is exceedingly deficient.*

Occasionally, in some of the more respectable districts, there are still to be found one or two of the old primitive Dame Schools, kept by a tidy, elderly female whose school has an appearance of neatness and order which strongly distinguishes it from the generality of this class of schools. The terms, however, are here somewhat higher, and the children evidently belong to a more respectable class of parents.

The terms of Dame Schools vary from 2d. to 7d. a week, and

thing there, the dames themselves naturally regard these schools and all similar innovations with a very hostile eye, as encroaching on their province, and likely, before very long, to break up their trade entirely.

* One of the best of these schools is kept by a blind man, who hears his scholars their lessons, and explains them with great simplicity, he is however liable to interruption in his academic labors, as his wife keeps a mangle, and he is obliged to turn it for her.

average 4d. The average yearly receipts of each Mistress are about £17. 16s.

The number of children attending these Dame Schools is 4,722; but it appears to the Committee that no instruction really deserving the name, is received in them; and in reckoning the number of those to be considered as partaking of the advantages of useful education, these children must be left almost entirely out of the account.

COMMON DAY SCHOOLS

These schools seem to be in rather better condition than those last mentioned, but are still very little fitted to give a really useful education to the children of the lower classes. The Masters are generally in no way qualified for their occupation;* take little interest in it, and show very little disposition to

* The masters themselves have generally a better opinion of their own qualifications for their office. One of them observed, during a visit paid to his school, that there were too many schools to do any good, adding, "I wish government would pass a law, that nobody but *them as is high larnt* should keep school, and then *we* might stand a chance to do some good."

Most of the Masters and Mistresses of these schools seemed to be strongly impressed with the superiority of their own plans to those of any other school, and were very little inclined to listen to any suggestions respecting improvements in the system of education that had been made in other places.—"The old road is the best," they would sometimes say. One master stated, that he had adopted a system which he thought would at once supply the great desiderata in education—"it is simply," he said, "in watching the dispositions of the children, and putting them especially to that particular thing which they take to." In illustration of this system, he called upon a boy about ten years of age, who had *taken to* Hebrew, and was just beginning to learn it: the Master acknowledging that he himself was learning too, in order to teach his pupil. On being asked whether he did not now and then find a few who did not *take to* any thing, he acknowledged that it was so; and this, he said, was the only weak point in his system, as he feared that he should not be able to make much of those children.

One of these Masters, who was especially conscious of the superior excellence of his establishment, as soon as he was acquainted with the object of the visit, began to dilate upon the various sciences with which he was familiar; among which he enumerated Hydraulics, Hydrostatics, Geography, Etymology, and Entomology. It was suggested to him that they had better perhaps take the list of queries in their order. On coming to the subjects taught in the schools, he was asked—Do you teach Reading and Writing?—

adopt any of the improvements that have elsewhere been made in the system of instruction. The terms are generally low, and it is no uncommon thing to find the Master professing to regulate his exertions by the rate of payment received from his pupils,— saying that he gives enough for 4d., 6d. or 8d., a-week; but that if the scholars would pay higher, he should teach them more. The payments vary from 3d. to 1s. 6d. per week, the greater number being from 6d. to 9d.; and the average receipts of the Masters are 16s. or 17s. a-week.

Though the schools in the accompanying tables are classed as Girls' and Boys' Schools, there are very few in which the sexes are entirely divided; almost every Boys' School containing some girls, and every Girls' School a few boys. They are chiefly the children of mechanics, warehousemen, or small shopkeepers, and learn reading, writing, and arithmetic; and in a very few of the better description of schools, a little grammar and geography.

In the great majority of these schools there seems to be a complete want of order and system.* The confusion arising from this defect, added to the very low qualifications of the Master,

Yes! Arithmetic?—Yes! Grammar and Composition?—Certainly! French? —Yes! Latin?—Yes! Greek?—Yes, yes! Geography?—Yes, etc.; and so on till the list of Queries was exhausted, answering every question in the affirmative. As he concluded the visitor remarked, "This is *multum in parvo* indeed," to which the Master immediately replied, "Yes, I teach that: you may put that down too."

* In one of these seminaries of learning, where there were about 130 children, the noise and confusion was so great as to render the replies of the Master to the enquiries put to him totally inaudible; he made several attempts to obtain silence but without effect; at length, as a last effort, he ascended his desk, and striking it forcibly with a ruler, said, in a strong Hibernian accent, "I'll tell you what it is, boys, the first I hear make a noise, I'll call him up, and kill him entirely;" and then perceiving probably on the countenance of his visitor some expression of dismay at this murderous threat, he added quickly in a more subdued tone, "almost I will." His menace produced no more effect than his previous appeals had done. A dead silence succeeded for a minute or two; then the whispering recommenced, and the talking, shuffling of feet, and general disturbance was soon as bad as ever. The Master gave up the point, saying as he descended from the desk, "You see the brutes, there's no managing them!"

the number of scholars under the superintendence of *one* Teacher, the irregularity of attendance, the great deficiency of books, and the injudicious plans of instruction, or rather the want of any plan, render them nearly inefficient for any purposes of real education.

Religious instruction is seldom attended to, beyond the rehearsal of a catechism; and moral education, real cultivation of mind, and improvement of character, are totally neglected. "Morals!" said one Master, in answer to the enquiry whether he taught them. "Morals! How am I to teach morals to the like of these?"*

The Girls' Schools are generally in much better condition than the Boys' Schools, and have a greater appearance of cleanliness, order and regularity. This seems to arise in part from the former being more constantly employed, and the scholars being fewer in number to each Teacher. *Report of a Committee of the Manchester Statistical Society on the State of Education in the Borough of Manchester in 1834* (2nd ed, 1837)

* The Committee met with two instances of schools kept by Masters of some abilities, but much given to drinking, who had however gained such a reputation, in their neighbourhood, that after spending a week or a fortnight in this pastime they could always fill their school-rooms again as soon as they returned to their post. The children during the absence of the Masters go to other schools for the week, or play in the streets, or are employed by their parents, in running errands, etc. On another occasion, one of these Instructors and Guardians of the morals of our youth, was met issuing from his school room at the head of his scholars to see a *fight* in the neighbourhood; and instead of stopping to reply to any educational queries, only uttered a breathless invitation to come along and see the sport.

PART FOUR

Government Involvement

In 1833 the British government decided that annual grants of £20,000 should be paid to denominational schools. The Committee of Council on Education was established in 1839 to ensure that the grant was spent effectively; inspectors were appointed to visit schools receiving a grant (24) and in 1846 the Committee of Council began to offer financial inducements to persuade schools to raise their teaching standards (25). Government expenditure thereafter rose, and by the middle of the century was nearly £200,000 per annum.

The combined efforts of church and government had made possible at least a little day schooling for nearly all children, most of it in the Church of England schools (26). But despite the dramatic expansion of educational facilities over the 1830s, 1840s and 1850s, the monitorial system lingered on (27). Herbert Spencer led the movement to replace the mechanical, rote-learning methods of utilitarian education with something more meaningful to children (28).

Government expenditure was over £700,000 in 1858 and a Royal Commission was appointed in that year to investigate the whole question of government investment in education. By the time it reported, in 1861, expenditure was over £800,000 (29). Anxious to economise, the government implemented one of the recommendations of the Royal Commission (or Newcastle Commission, as it is known), namely the recommendation suggesting that schools and teachers should be paid "by results" (30). Another recommendation adopted was the drastic pruning of the syllabus (31). Payment by results had its critics (32) but the majority of inspectors thought the new policy was an improvement (33). Even its severest critic, Matthew Arnold, conceded that payment by results had improved the school readers (34).

24 Sir James Kay Shuttleworth   Government inspection

The government began paying grants to schools in 1833. From 1839 it made grants conditional upon inspection by the newly established Committee of Privy Council on Education. Dr James Kay (later known as Sir James Kay Shuttleworth), the first secretary of the Committee, issued detailed instructions to his school inspectors.

INSTRUCTIONS FOR THE INSPECTORS
OF SCHOOLS

THE Lords of the Committee of Council on Education consider that the duties of the Inspectors of Schools may be divided into *three distinct branches*.

1st. Those duties relate, in the first place, to inquiry in neighbourhoods from whence applications have been made for aid to erect new schools, in order to enable the Committee of Council to determine the propriety of granting funds in aid of the expenses proposed to be incurred, or to the examination of certain special cases in which claims of peculiar urgency are advanced for temporary aid in the support and improvement of existing schools.

2ndly. To the inspection of the several schools aided by public grants issued under the authority of the Committee, and an examination of the method and matter of instruction, and the character of the discipline established in them, so as to enable the Inspector to report thereon to this Committee, for the information of both Houses of Parliament.

3dly. As incidental to and in furtherance of these duties, Inspectors may also be required by the Committee to make inquiries respecting the state of elementary education in particular districts.

FIRSTLY

When cases are referred to the Inspector belonging to the first head of inquiry, he will bear in mind that the grant of the last Session is to be chiefly applied in aid of subscription for building; and, in particular and special cases, in aid of the support of schools connected with the National Society and the British and Foreign School Society.

The Committee furnish the Inspectors with a copy of the Order in Council of the 3d of June, and with the annexed regulations of the 24th of September, by which the appropriation of the Parliamentary grant made in the late session will be determined.

In the first class of cases, the Inspector will be careful to obtain as precise information as possible respecting the intentions of the promoters of the intended school in relation to each of the regulations of the 24th September, and to each of the questions in the Form (A.) (appended hereto), respecting the site and structure of the school-house, and the reasons for expecting that the school will be efficiently and permanently supported. He will forward a plan of the building proposed to be erected, containing the dimensions and height of the rooms, and specifying the appropriation of each part. In the school-rooms, sectional drawings must be given of the position of the desks and forms as proposed to be arranged on the floor. The Inspector will ascertain whether any ground, and to what extent, is to be appropriated to the recreation of the children, how it will be enclosed, and whether it is intended to furnish it with the means of exercise and recreation; and whenever his advice is sought he will encourage the adoption of such arrangements. If the schoolmaster's house do not form part of the building, the Inspector will ascertain whether it is situated in the immediate vicinity of the school, or at what distance. The plans of school-houses, prepared by the direction of this committee, will always be available for such promoters of schools as may be desirous to adopt the arrangements suggested by the most extensive experience. The Inspector will personally ascertain all circumstances affecting the healthfulness of the site; as, for example, its drainage, ventilation, the proximity of any stagnant water, or of any establishments which may be injurious to health.

The probable amount of stipend proposed to be raised by subscription, or from endowment, or annual collections, together with the amount of school fees likely to be collected from the parents of the children, with other allowances or emoluments, ought to be such as will enable a well-qualified schoolmaster to live in comfort and respectability, if he devote his whole time to the duties of his vocation; and will therefore be a subject of special inquiry to the Inspector.

He will also report on the funds available for the provision of books and school apparatus, and on the views of the promoters of the school respecting the extent of instruction which they wish to be imparted, and the nature of the discipline which they desire to be pursued in the school. He will ascertain whether any and what arrangements are made for the practical instruction of the girls in household management, and whether the instruction of the boys will have a practical relation to their probable future employment.

In relation to the 3d clause of the 4th regulation of the 24th September, requiring "that the site of the school-house shall be obtained, with a good legal tenure, and that, by conveyance to trustees, it has been duly secured for the education of the children of the poor," the Inspectors are furnished with a copy of the 6th & 7th William IV., cap. 70, intituled, "An Act to facilitate the Conveyance of the Sites of School-houses," and with the instructions issued by the National Society, and the forms provided for this purpose by the British and Foreign School Society, as well as with forms prepared under the direction of the Committee of Council, in order to meet the wants of the promoters of some other classes of schools.

The 9th regulation of the 24th September requires, "that in

every application for aid to the erection of a school-house in England and Wales, it must be stated whether the school is in connexion with the National Society or with the British and Foreign School Society; and if the said school be not in connexion with either of those societies, the Committee will not entertain the case unless some special circumstances be stated to induce their Lordships to treat the case as special." The Inspectors will occasionally have to examine the special representations made in such cases; and when the case appears to the Committee to warrant further investigation, the Inspectors may have to conduct the inquiries contained in the extract from the minutes of the 3d December (in the Appendix to these instructions), respecting the arrangements which the school committee or chief promoters of such schools propose to make, for conducting the religious instruction in an efficient manner; to ascertain whether the Bible will be read daily in the school, and what means are to be adopted to secure from the children attending the school an observance of religious duties, and attendance on divine worship, having a due regard to the rights of conscience.

Cases of peculiar urgency, arising in poor and populous neighbourhoods, in which representations are made of the want of the means of elementary education, and the absolute dependence of the population, from extreme poverty, on the public aid for the provision of schools, will sometimes be referred to the Inspectors for examination, before the Committee determine whether more than the ordinary amount of assistance shall be granted. Such inquiries will sometimes require a general survey of the condition of the poor in the vicinity, and particularly of the extent and quality of the existing means of elementary education; and the Inspector will be furnished with tabular forms in which to collect and combine the facts ascertained by such inquiries.

Well-conducted schools may, at particular periods, be subject to embarrassment from the death or removal of some patron who has provided a considerable portion of the annual

income of the school, or from some local disaster, occasioning
the withdrawal of the usual resources on which the school has
been dependent, or from other similar causes, in which "peculiar cases, temporary aid may be sought to meet the annual
expenses of existing schools:" the personal examination of the
school by the Inspectors, to test the efficiency of the management, will be required in the majority of such applications; and
they will find in another part of these instructions full information respecting the nature of the inquiries to be made in such
cases, and tabular forms in which to collect the results of their
inspection. The efficiency of the school management having
been ascertained, the Inspector will inquire whether all other
efforts to obtain resources for the support of the school have
been exhausted, and whether there is a reasonable prospect that
temporary aid from the Parliamentary grant would enable the
promoters of the school to ensure its future permanent efficiency, without the necessity of renewing their application;
such assistance being always regarded as an exception to
general rules, and to be granted only in cases in which the
strongest evidence of its necessity and utility is afforded.

SECONDLY

In proceeding to inspect the method and matter of instruction, and the character of the discipline established in the
several schools aided by the grants of this Committee, the Inspector will bear in mind that his visit will prove of much
greater value to the school, if he is accompanied by the committee, or chief promoters of the school, in his examination of
the children; inasmuch as all permanent improvements must
depend, for the most part, on the exertions of the Committee or
chief promoters of the school. He will therefore generally an-
nounce his visit to the parochial clergyman, or other minister of
religion, connected with the school, or to the chairman or
secretary of the school committee, and proceed to examine the
school in their presence. He will abstain from any interference
with the instruction, management, or discipline of the school,

and will on all occasions carefully avoid any act which could tend to impair the authority of the school committee or chief promoters of the school over the teacher or over the children, or of the teacher himself over his scholars. He will receive from them any communication which they may wish to make, and afford them such assistance and information as they may be desirous to obtain.

Having inspected the state of the boundary fences, exercise-ground, external walls, roof, etc., and ascertained whether the premises are in good repair, the other subjects of inquiry naturally arrange themselves under the following heads and subdivisions.

The Committee of Council, in placing these subjects of inquiry in the hands of the Inspector, by no means expect he will find that the several objects of education adverted to in them are attained in every school. The inquiries relate to different methods of instruction, and to all the subjects of instruction taught under such methods; a comprehensive series of questions is on this account necessary. These questions, moreover, are not to be received as an indication, in any respect, of what the Committee of Council consider desirable, either as respects the method or the matter of instruction, but as a mode of collecting the facts of each case, and as a catalogue of methods pursued, and of things taught under certain varieties of elementary instruction, but which are not found united in any one school, because some of them are incompatible with each other.

Neither is the Inspector to receive those inquiries as an exposition of the extent to which, in the opinion of the Committee, intellectual instruction should proceed, but simply as an indication of the facts which he may have occasion to record. . . . *Minutes of the Committee of Council on Education* (1839–40), 19–22

---

25 The pupil teacher scheme

In 1846 the Committee of Council on Education took a major step towards replacing the monitorial system. Grants were allocated for able children to carry on for five extra years at school as paid monitors or pupil teachers.

_____

COUNCIL CHAMBER, WHITEHALL,
21st December, 1846.
By the Right Honourable the Lords of the Committee of Council on Education
REGULATIONS respecting the EDUCATION of PUPIL TEACHERS and STIPENDIARY MONITORS
THE Lord President communicated to their Lordships the Regulations which he had caused to be framed to carry into execution the Minute of the Committee of Council on Education of the 25th day of August, 1846, respecting the Apprenticeship of Pupil Teachers.

General Preliminary Conditions

Upon application being made to their Lordships from the trustees or managers of any school under inspection, requesting that one or more of the most proficient scholars be selected to be apprenticed to the master or mistress, the application will be referred to the Inspector, and will be entertained, if he report,—

That the master or mistress of the school is competent to conduct the apprentice through the course of instruction to be required:

That the school is well furnished and well supplied with books and apparatus:

That it is divided into classes; and that the instruction is skilful, and is graduated according to the age of the children and the time they have been at school, so as to show that equal care has been bestowed on each class:

That the discipline is mild and firm, and conducive to good order:

That there is a fair prospect that the salary of the master and mistress, and the ordinary expenses of the school, will be provided for during the period of apprenticeship.

General Rule.—The qualifications to be required of candidates and of pupil teachers in each year of their apprenticeship will be regulated by the following rules, in which the minimum of proficiency to be attained is precisely defined, in order to prevent partiality; but their Lordships reserve to themselves the power to reward superior merit by shortening the term of the apprenticeship, or by awarding the higher stipends of the later years of the apprenticeship to pupil teachers whose attainments enable them to pass the examination of one of the later years at an earlier period.

Pupil Teachers.—Qualifications of Candidates

The following qualifications will be required from candidates for apprenticeship:—

They must be at least thirteen years of age, and must not be subject to any bodily infirmity likely to impair their usefulness as pupil teachers.

In schools connected with the Church of England, the clergyman and managers, and, in other schools, the managers, must certify that the moral character of the candidates and of their families justify an expectation that the instruction and training of the school will be seconded by their own efforts and by the example of their parents. If this cannot be certified of the family, the apprentice will be required to board in some approved household.

Candidates will also be required,—

1. To read with fluency, ease, and expression.

2. To write in a neat hand, with correct spelling and punctuation, a simple prose narrative slowly read to them.

3. To write from dictation sums in the first four rules of arithmetic, simple and compound; to work them correctly, and to know the tables of weights and measures.

4. To point out the parts of speech in a simple sentence.

5. To have an elementary knowledge of geography.

6. *In schools connected with the Church of England* they will be required to repeat the Catechism, and to show that they understand its meaning, and are acquainted with the outline of

Scripture history. The parochial clergyman will assist in this part of the examination.

In other schools the state of the religious knowledge will be certified by the managers.

7. To teach a junior class to the satisfaction of the Inspector.

8. Girls should also be able to sew neatly and to knit.

Qualifications of Pupil Teachers in each Year of their Apprenticeship

At the end of the first year pupil teachers will be examined by the Inspector:—

1. In writing from memory the substance of a more difficult narrative.

2. In arithmetic, the rules of "Practice" and "Simple Proportion,*" and in the first rules* of mental arithmetic.

3. In grammar, in the construction of sentences, and in syntax.

4. In the geography of Great Britain and Palestine.

5. In the Holy Scriptures and in the Catechism, with illustrations by passages from Holy Writ, *in Church of England schools*, the parochial clergyman assisting in the examination.

The managers will, *in other schools*, certify in this and in the succeeding years of the apprenticeship, that they are satisfied with the state of the religious knowledge of the pupil teachers.

6. In their ability to give a class a reading lesson, and to examine it on the meaning of what has been read.

7. In the elements of vocal music, in this and in succeeding years, when taught from notes.

8. In their ability to drill* a class in marching and exercises; and to conduct it through the class movements required for preserving order.

9. Girls should also be able to instruct the younger scholars in sewing and knitting.

At the end of the second year, pupil teachers will be examined by the Inspector:—

1. In composition, by writing the *abstract of a lesson, or a school report.

2. In decimal arithmetic,* and the higher rules of mental arithmetic. Girls will not be required to proceed beyond the rule of "Compound Proportion" in this year.

3. In syntax and etymology.*

4. In the geography of Great Britain, of Europe, the British empire,* and Palestine.

5. In the Holy Scriptures, Liturgy, and Catechism *in Church of England schools,* more fully than in the preceding year, the parochial clergyman assisting in the examination.

6. In their ability to examine a class in reading, in the rudiments of grammar and arithmetic; and during the examination, to keep the class attentive, in order, and in activity without undue noise.

At the end of the third year, pupil teachers will be examined by the Inspector:—

1. In the composition of the notes of a lesson on a subject selected by the Inspector.

2. In the elements of mechanics,* or in book-keeping.

3. In syntax, etymology, and prosody.*

4. In the geography of the four* quarters of the globe. Girls in the geography of the British Empire.

5. In the outlines of English history.

6. More fully in the Holy Scriptures, Liturgy, and Catechism, *in Church of England schools,* the parochial clergyman assisting in the examination.

7. In their skill in managing and examining the second class in grammar, geography, and mental arithmetic.

8. The girls should have acquired greater skill as teachers of sewing, knitting, etc.

At the end of the fourth year, pupil teachers will be examined by the Inspector:—

H

1. In the composition of an account of the organization of the school, and of the methods of instruction used.

2. In the first steps in mensuration,* with practical illustrations; and in the elements of land surveying*and levelling.*

3. In syntax, etymology, and prosody.*

4. In the *geography of Great Britain as connected with the outlines of English history. Girls in the geography of the four quarters of the globe.

5. More fully in the Holy Scriptures, Liturgy, and Catechism, *in Church of England schools,* the parochial clergyman assisting in the examination.

6. In their skill in managing and examining the first class in grammar, geography, and mental arithmetic, and in giving* a lesson to two or three classes grouped together.

At the end of the fifth year, pupil teachers will be examined by the Inspector:—

1. In the composition of an essay on some subject connected with the art of teaching.

2. In the rudiments of algebra,* or the practice of land surveying* and levelling*.

3. In syntax, etymology, and prosody.

4. In the use* of the globes, or in the geography of the British empire* and Europe,* as connected with the outlines of English history. In this year girls may be examined in the historical geography of Great Britain.

5. More completely in the Holy Scriptures, Liturgy, and Catechism, *in Church of England schools,* the parochial clergyman assisting in the examination.

6. In their ability to give a gallery lesson, and to conduct the instruction of the first class in any subject selected by the Inspector.

General Rules.—In the subjects marked with an asterisk girls need not be examined, but in every year they will be expected to show increased skill as sempstresses, and teachers of sewing, knitting, etc.

In the examinations, the Inspectors will, in each year, observe the degree of attention paid by the pupil teachers to a perfect articulation in reading, and to a right modulation of the voice in teaching a class. A knowledge of vocal music and of drawing (especially from models), though not absolutely required, because the means of teaching it may not exist in every school, will be much encouraged. Every pupil teacher will be required to be clean in person and dress.

The number of pupil teachers apprenticed in any school will not exceed one to every twenty-five scholars ordinarily attending.

Certificate.—Every pupil teacher who has passed all the foregoing examinations, and has presented the required testimonials in each year, will be entitled to a certificate declaring that he has successfully completed his apprenticeship. . . .

. . .   *Certificates of Character and Conduct to be annually*
required from Pupil Teachers and Stipendiary Monitors

At the close of each year pupil teachers or stipendiary monitors will be required to present certificates of good conduct from the managers of the school, and of punctuality, diligence, obedience, and attention to their duties from the master or mistress.

In Church of England schools, the parochial clergyman, and *in other schools*, the managers, will also certify that the pupil teachers or stipendiary monitors have been attentive to their religious duties.

Salaries of Pupil Teachers and Stipendiary Monitors

If these certificates be presented, and if the inspector certify, at the close of each year, that he is satisfied with the oral examination and the examination papers of the pupil teachers or stipendiary monitors, and if those papers be satisfactory to their Lordships, the following stipends will be paid, irrespectively of any sum that may be received from the school or from any other source:—

							For a Pupil Teacher		For a Stipendiary Monitor	
							£.	s.	£.	s.
At the end of the	1st	Year	..	..	10	0	..	5	0
„	„	„	2nd	„	..	..	12	10	..	7	10
„	„	„	3rd	„	..	..	15	0	..	10	0
„	„	„	4th	„	..	..	17	10	..	12	10
„	„	„	5th	„	..	..	20	0	..	0	0

Remuneration and Duties of Schoolmasters and Mistresses

At the close of each of these years, if the pupil teachers have received a certificate of good character and of satisfactory progress, the master or mistress by whom they have been instructed and trained shall be paid the sum of 5*l.* for one, of 9*l.* for two, of 12*l.* for three pupil teachers, and 3*l.* per annum more for every additional apprentice; and, on the like conditions, 2*l.* 10s. for one stipendiary monitor, 4*l.* for two, 6*l.* for three, and 1*l.* 10s. in addition in each year for every additional stipendiary monitor.

In addition to the foregoing subjects of instruction, if the pupil teachers be skilfully trained by the master in the culture of a garden, or in some mechanical arts suitable to a school of industry, or the female pupil teachers be instructed by the mistress in cutting out clothes, and in cooking, baking, or washing, as well as in the more usual arts of sewing and knitting, and the Inspector certify that the pupil teachers are thereby in a satisfactory course of training for the management of a school of industry, the master or mistress will receive an additional gratuity, proportioned to the degree of skill and care displayed.

In consideration of the foregoing gratuity, and of the assistance obtained from the pupil teachers and stipendiary monitors in the instruction and management of the school, the master will give them instruction in the prescribed subjects, during one hour and a half at least, during five days in the week, either before or after the usual hours of school-keeping.

The stipends will be liable to be withdrawn by their Lordships on the report of their Inspector, on proof, of the continued

TABLE B.

CLASSIFICATION OF DAY SCHOOLS.
(according to their Sources of Maintenance.)

SUMMARY OF ENGLAND AND WALES.

DESCRIPTION OF SCHOOLS.	No. of Schools*.	Number of Scholars belonging to the Schools.†			DESCRIPTION OF SCHOOLS.	No. of Schools.	Number of Scholars belonging to the Schools.		
		Both Sexes.	M.	F.			Both Sexes.	M.	F.
ALL DAY SCHOOLS	44,836	2,108,592	1,139,324	969,268	CLASS III.—cont. *Denominational*—cont.				
					Moravians - - -	7	366	218	148
PUBLIC DAY SCHOOLS -	15,411	1,413,170	795,632	617,538	Wesleyan Methodists— British	20	3,082	1,805	1,277
PRIVATE DAY SCHOOLS -	29,425	695,422	343,692	351,730	„ Others	343	36,682	22,635	14,047
					Methodist New Con- nexion— British	3	667	450	217
Classification of Public Schools.					„ Others	10	1,148	618	530
CLASS I.—SUPPORTED BY GENERAL OR LOCAL TAXATION - - -	610	48,826	28,708	20,118	Primitive Methodists— British	2	206	103	103
					„ Others	23	1,091	520	571
CLASS II.—SUPPORTED BY ENDOWMENTS - -	3,125	206,279	138,495	67,784	Bible Christians— British	1	64	26	38
					„ Others	7	303	171	132
CLASS III. — SUPPORTED BY RELIGIOUS BODIES -	10,595	1,048,851	569,300	479,551	Wesleyan Methodist Association	10	1,112	616	496
					Calvinistic Methodists— British	22	1,759	1,085	674
CLASS IV.—OTHER PUB- LIC SCHOOLS - -	1,081	109,214	59,129	50,085	„ Others	19	1,055	599	456
					Lady Huntingdon's Con- nexion – British	1	80	..	80
CLASS I.					„ Others	8	564	306	258
Military Schools - -	35	3,348	2,560	788	New Church Dissenters (not defined)	9	1,551	891	660
Naval Schools - -	14	2,348	1,963	385	– British	28	3,851	2,398	1,453
Woods and Forests School	1	259	135	124	„ Others	15	1,541	861	680
Corporation Schools –	3	2,394	1,364	1,030	Lutherans – -	1	157	107	50
Workhouse Schools - -	523	38,067	20,660	17,407	French Protestants -	1	15	..	15
Prison Schools - -	34	2,410	2,026	384	German Missionary Society –	1	100	40	60
CLASS II.					Isolated Congrega- tions— British	2	184	130	54
Collegiate and Grammar Schools - - -	566	35,612	32,221	3,391	Roman Catholics - -	311	38,583	20,501	18,082
Other Endowed Schools ‡ -	2,559	170,667	106,274	64,393	Jews - - -	10	1,234	735	499
CLASS III.					*Undenominational.*				
Denominational.					British - - -	514	82,597	52,037	30,560
Ch. of England— National	3,720	464,975	253,934	211,041	Others - - -	4	1,062	532	510
„ British	12	1,043	600	443	CLASS IV.				
„ Others	4,839	335,489	169,206	166,283	Ragged Schools (*exclusive of those supported by religious bodies*) § -	123	22,337	12,705	9,632
Ch. of Scotland— British	1	130	130	..	Orphan Schools - -	39	3,764	1,712	2,052
„ Others	4	816	522	294	Blind Schools - -	11	609	342	267
United Presbyterians -	3	217	148	69	Deaf and Dumb Schools –	9	392	202	190
Presbyterian Church in England— British	2	86	48	38	School for Idiots - -	1	18	16	2
„ Others	23	2,361	1,501	860	Factory Schools - -	115	17,834	9,724	8,110
Scottish Presbyterians	1	345	195	150	Colliery Schools - -	41	3,511	2,013	1,498
Presbyterians (not otherwise defined)— British	1	263	143	120	Chemical Works Schools -	4	832	433	399
„ Others	6	1,058	607	451	Foundry School - -	1	103	55	48
Independents —British	183	22,598	12,586	10,012	Mechanics' Institution Schools - -	5	1,564	1,223	341
„ Others	248	24,808	13,833	10,975	Industrial Schools - -	6	607	383	224
Baptists— British	51	4,946	2,895	2,051	Agricultural Schools	3	264	203	61
„ Others	64	3,719	1,861	1,858	Railway Schools - -	5	842	440	402
Society of Friends— British	5	577	247	330	Philanthropic Society's Farm School - -	1	96	96	..
„ Others	18	1,870	990	680	Other Subscription Schools of no specific character—	717	56,441	29,582	26,859
Unitarians— British	4	882	649	233					
„ Others	26	2,854	1,322	1,532	Total of British Schools of all Descriptions	852	123,015	75,332	47,683

* By the term "school" is here meant a distinct establishment; thus, a school for boys and girls, if under one general management and conducted in one range of building is regarded as only one school, although the tuition may be carried on in separate compartments of the building, under separate superintendence.

† It has not been thought necessary to encumber these Tables with the number of scholars *attending* each class of day schools. The total number attending all private schools and the aggregate of public schools is given in the previous summary (Table A.); and there is nothing to lead to the conclusion that the proportion of attendance is materially greater in one class of public schools than in another. See the facts given respecting two counties; *post*, page cxxxviii.

‡ For a minuter classification of these schools, see Supplement I. to Table B., page cxxiv.

§ The total number of Ragged Schools is 132, containing 23,643 scholars.

ill health of the pupil teachers or stipendiary monitors, or of misconduct, want of punctuality, diligence, or skill, or failure in their examination, or in default of the required certificates. *Parliamentary Papers*, XLV (1847), 3–7

26 1851 Census of Education

This was the first comprehensive survey of English and Welsh educational facilities. Two important facts emerge: most children were receiving some day school education by 1851, and an overwhelming majority attended Church of England schools. Figures under 'number of scholars belonging to the schools', however, are exaggerated. (Table, p 117.)

27 Ruminating animals

The monitorial system was disappearing in the 1850s but its traditions lingered. Teachers were allowed little freedom, as we can judge from the following specimen lesson. It is the style ridiculed by Dickens in *Hard Times*.

CLASS TEACHING—INTERROGATION

The mode of conducting interrogative exercises may be best shown by a specimen; one, therefore, is given on a paragraph taken from the lesson book.

SPECIMEN LESSON ON INTERROGATION
Daily Lesson Book, No. IV., pp. 76, 77.

RUMINATING ANIMALS.—Cud-chewing or ruminating animals form the *eighth* order. These, with the exception of the camel, having no cutting teeth in the upper jaw, but their place is supplied with a hard pad. In the lower jaw there are eight cutters; the tearers, in general, are absent, so that there is a vacant space between the cutters and grinders. The latter are very broad, and are kept rough and fit for grinding the vegetable food on which these animals live, by the enamel being disposed in crescent-shaped ridges.

The great peculiarity of the cud-chewers is the power which they possess of bringing back the food into the mouth, after it has been swallowed, to be further masticated. They have four stomachs, and very long intestines; vegetable food requiring to be kept in the body for a longer period than animal food.

The fore feet, having nothing whatever to do with the food, are not adapted either for feeling or seizing, but simply, like the hind feet, for giving support. They are composed of a solid horny substance, divided into two parts; hence these animals are sometimes called cloven-footed animals.

This order is divided into two families, viz., hornless and horned animals. In the first family are the camel and musk, and the second includes deer, sheep, goats, antelopes, giraffes, and oxen. These animals are more useful to man than any others; many of them draw and carry burdens, and nearly all are used for food.

Teacher. "What have you been reading about?"

Pupil. "Ruminating animals."

Teacher: "Give me another name for ruminating."

Pupil. "Cud-chewing."

Teacher: "What is the root of the word?"

Pupil. "Rumen, the cud."

Teacher. "What does the termination *ate* mean?"

Pupil. "To do or act on in some way.

Teacher. "Ruminate, then, is to——"

Pupil. "To act on the cud."

Teacher. "What *division* of animals do the cud-chewing form?"

Pupil. "The eighth order."

Teacher. "Of what class?"

Pupil. "Of the class Mammalia."

Teacher. "What is the class Mammalia?"

Pupil. "It includes all animals that bring forth their young alive."

Teacher. "Next boy."

Second Pupil. "And that suckle their young."

Teacher: "To which of the sub-kingdoms of nature does the class Mammalia belong?"
Pupil. "To the sub-kingdom Vertebrata."
Teacher. "How many orders has this class Mammalia?"
Pupil. "Nine."
Teacher. "Name the first order."
Pupil. "Two-handed animals."
Teacher. "Give me an example."
Pupil. "Man is the only one."
Teacher. "Name the second."
Pupil. "Four-handed animals."
Teacher. "Give me an example."
Pupil. "The monkey."
Teacher. "Name the third order."
Pupil. "Killing animals."
Teacher. "Give me an example."
Pupil. "The lion."
Teacher. "Name the fourth order."
Pupil. "Pouched animals."
Teacher. "Give me an example."
Pupil. "The kangaroo."
Teacher. "Name the fifth order."
Pupil. "Gnawing animals."
Teacher. "Give me an example." . . .

A Hand-book to the Borough Road Schools; explanatory of the Methods of Instruction adopted by the British and Foreign School Society (1854), 40–1

---

28 Herbert Spencer   Education and the laws of life
Though rote learning was still in vogue in the 1860s, it did not go unchallenged. The influential and widely read philosopher Herbert Spencer (1820–1903) had his *Education, Intellectual, Moral and Physical* published in 1861. Here he is attacking the narrowness of the average school curriculum.

We are quite prepared to hear from many that all this is throwing away time and energy; and that children would be much better occupied in writing their copies or learning their pence-tables, and so fitting themselves for the business of life. We regret that such crude ideas of what constitutes education, and such a narrow conception of utility, should still be prevalent. Saying nothing on the need for a systematic culture of the perceptions and the value of the practices above inculcated as subserving that need, we are prepared to defend them even on the score of the knowledge gained. If men are to be mere cits, mere porers over ledgers, with no ideas beyond their trades— if it is well that they should be as the cockney whose conception of rural pleasures extends no further than sitting in a tea-garden smoking pipes and drinking porter; or as the squire who thinks of woods as places for shooting in, of uncultivated plants as nothing but weeds, and who classifies animals into game, vermin, and stock—then indeed it is needless to learn anything that does not directly help to replenish the till and fill the larder. But if there is a more worthy aim for us than to be drudges—if there are other uses in the things around us than their power to bring money—if there are higher faculties to be exercised than acquisitive and sensual ones—if the pleasures which poetry and art and science and philosophy can bring are of any moment; then is it desirable that the instinctive inclination which every child shows to observe natural beauties and investigate natural phenomena, should be encouraged. But this gross utilitarianism which is content to come into the world and quit it again without knowing what kind of a world it is or what it contains, may be met on its own ground. It will by and by be found that a knowledge of the laws of life is more important than any other knowledge whatever—that the laws of life underlie not only all bodily and mental processes, but by implication all the transactions of the house and the street, all commerce, all politics, all morals—and that therefore without a comprehension of them, neither personal nor social conduct can be rightly regulated. It will eventually be seen too, that the laws of life are essentially the same throughout the whole organic creation; and further, that they cannot be properly understood in their complex manifestations until they have been studied in their simpler ones. And when this is seen, it will be also seen that in aiding the child to acquire the out-of-door information for which it shows so great an avidity, and in encouraging the acquisition of such information throughout youth, we are simply inducing it to store up the raw material of future organization—the facts that will one day bring home to it with due force, those great generalizations of science by which actions may be rightly guided. . . . Herbert Spencer. *Education, Intellectual, Moral and Physical* (1905 ed), 105–6

29 The Newcastle Report

The rapidly rising educational expenditure alarmed the government. In 1858 it appointed a Royal Commission (the Newcastle Commission) to investigate the provision of a 'sound and cheap' system of elementary education. The Commission produced a detailed six-volume report covering all aspects of elementary education. The document that follows is the Commission's summary of its report.

Summary of Recommendations

We have now discharged the duty imposed upon us, have examined the condition of education among the poorer classes of Your Majesty's subjects, and have suggested means for its improvement in all its principal branches. We have given an account of the leading institutions, whether in connexion with the Government or with the great charitable societies of the country, by which the education of the poor is superintended and assisted, and have described the different classes of elementary schools. We have endeavoured to ascertain the general character and the ability of the teachers both in public and private schools and have particularly inquired into the education given to the pupils of the training colleges, who may justly be supposed to become the highest class of elementary teachers. We have followed these teachers, both public and private, to their schools, have tested the merits of their instruction and have inquired into the regularity of the attendance of the scholars. We have carried our inquiry beyond the limits of the schools for the independent poor into the schools for pauper children; into the factory and print-works schools; into the ragged, industrial, and reformatory schools; and into the schools maintained by the State both for children and adults in the Army and Navy. We have also caused a full Statistical Report to be prepared, containing details with regard to the numbers of children now under instruction, the sums expended on education, and other collateral subjects.

Our attention, however, has principally been devoted to the system of aid and inspection established by Your Majesty's Government, which has now for twenty years given a powerful stimulus to the building of schools, and has created a class of schoolmasters and pupil-teachers of a superior character to any previously known in this country. We have dwelt fully both on the merits and the defects of this system. We have found it stimulating voluntary subscriptions, offering many excellent models of teaching, and adapting itself to the character of the people by leaving both the general management of the schools and their religious teaching free. On the other hand we have exposed great and growing defects in its tendency to indefinite expense, in its inability to assist the poorer districts, in the partial inadequacy of its teaching, and in the complicated business which encumbers the central office of the Committee of Council; and these defects have led us to believe that any attempt to extend it unaltered into a national system would fail. We have therefore proposed, while retaining the leading principles of the present system and simplifying its working, to combine with it a supplementary and local system which may diffuse a wider interest in education, may distribute its burdens more equally, and may enable every school in the country to participate in its benefits.

In close connexion with the education of the independent

poor, we have proposed in another part of our Report a scheme by which the charities which have been given for purposes of education, and others which appear justly available for that object may be employed in a more advantageous manner than is possible at present under the limited powers of the Charity Commissioners.

Turning to the education of the children of other classes of the poor, we have shown with regard to the children of the in-door paupers, that while the intellectual teaching of many workhouse schools is good, great moral evil has resulted from educating children in close contact with adults many of whom are of a corrupted character; and we have at the same time pointed out the peculiar facilities for giving to such children a sound education, both moral and intellectual, which arise from the fact that their whole time and management are at the disposition of the guardians of the poor. We have also shown that a control of a beneficial kind may be exercised by the guardians over the children of parents in receipt of outdoor relief.

With regard to vagrant and criminal children, we have been led to think that, however desirable it may be that charitable persons should try every means for forcing education upon neglected and ignorant classes, ragged schools, unless affording industrial occupation, cannot be properly distinguished as objects for public assistance from other humble classes of schools for elementary instruction. We are of opinion that the education of children who are peculiarly in danger of becoming criminals would be most fitly conducted in district or separate pauper schools; but we recommend the continuance for the present of certified industrial schools, which have been attended with great success. Lastly, the success of the reformatory schools appears to us to indicate that schools of this description are best entrusted to the control of Government. In the State schools for the Military Service, we find a good system in operation. In the Naval Schools we find defects, remedies for which are recommended.

We now proceed to enumerate our principal recommendations.

I. PLAN FOR GIVING ASSISTANCE TO THE SCHOOLS OF THE INDEPENDENT POOR

1. That all assistance given to the annual maintenance of schools shall be simplified and reduced to grants of two kinds.

The first of these grants shall be paid out of the general taxation of the country, in consideration of the fulfilment of certain conditions by the managers of the schools. Compliance with these conditions is to be ascertained by the Inspectors.

The second shall be paid out of the county rates, in consideration of the attainment of a certain degree of knowledge by the children in the school during the year preceding the payment. The existence of this degree of knowledge shall be ascertained by examiners appointed by County and Borough Boards of Education herein-after described.

2. That no school shall be entitled to these grants which shall not fulfil the following general conditions.

The school shall have been registered at the office of the Privy Council, on the report of the Inspector, as an elementary school for the education of the poor.

The school shall be certified by the Inspector to be healthy and properly drained and ventilated, and supplied with offices; and the principal school-room shall contain at least eight square feet of superficial area for each child in average daily attendance.

3. That there shall be paid upon the average daily attendance of the children during the year preceding the inspector's visit as the Committee of Council shall fix from time to time, the sums specified in Part I., Chapter 6, for each child, according to the opinion formed by the Inspectors of the discipline, efficiency, and general character of the school.

4. That there shall also be paid an additional grant of 2s. 6d. a child on so many of the average number of children in attendance throughout the year as have been under the instruction of properly qualified pupil-teachers, or assistant teachers, allowing

30 children for each pupil-teacher, or 60 for each assistant teacher.

5. That every school which applies for aid out of the county rate shall be examined by a county examiner within 12 months after the application, in reading, writing, and arithmetic, and that any one of Her Majesty's Inspectors of Schools under whose inspection the school will fall shall be entitled to be present at the examination.

6. That, subject to recommendation 7, the managers of all schools fulfilling the conditions specified in Rule 3, shall be entitled to be paid out of the county rate a sum varying from 22s. 6d. to 21s. for every child who has attended the school during 140 days in the year preceding the day of examination, and who passes an examination before the examiner in reading, writing, arithmetic, and who, if a girl, also passes an examination in plain work. That scholars under 7 years of age shall not be examined, but the amount of the grant shall be determined by the average number of children in daily attendance, 20s. being paid on account of each child.

7. That the combined grants from the Central Fund and the County Board shall never exceed the fees and subscriptions, or 15s. per child on the average attendance. *Royal Commission on Popular Education*, Vol I, 542–5, 1861 [2794–1], XXI, Part I

30 Instructions to inspectors

The government, anxious to economise, decided to implement the most controversial recommendation of the Newcastle Commission, payment by results. The old grant system was swept away and schools were paid 4s for every child in attendance, plus 2s 8d per subject for every child who passed an annual examination in reading, writing and arithmetic. In the document below the Committee of Council instructs its inspectorate on the conduct of the examination.

. . . 13. It is assumed that you have before you the examination schedule filled up by the managers as far as column viii.

inclusive, and that the school is placed before you *in the order of its usual classes*. It may be well to test this by asking for the class registers, and calling over by it the names of two of the classes taken at a venture. It is also assumed that you have a paper before you containing the dictation which you mean to give for writing and arithmetic under each standard.

14. All the children will remain in their places throughout the examination.

15. You will begin with writing and arithmetic, and you will direct the teachers to see that all who are to be examined under standard I. have before them a slate and pencil, under standards II. and III. a slate, a pencil, and a reading book; all under standards IV.–VI., a half sheet of folio paper, a pen, ink and the appropriate reading book.

16. You will then call "Standard I., stand up throughout the school." The children answering to this description will stand up in their usual places without quitting them. The object of the movement is to ascertain those who are to act on your next order without destroying the daily arrangement of the school. When this has been correctly effected by the assistance of the teachers, you will call "Standard I., sit down, and write on your slates as I dictate."

17. You will then dictate the letters and figures which they are to write down.

You will pursue the same course with standard II, directing them to write their names and standard on their slates, and announcing to them out of their book the line they are to copy, and their sums.

You will pursue the same course, *mutatis mutandis*, with standards III. (slates), and IV.–VI. (paper).

18. The whole school having thus had their dictation given to them, and being at work on their arithmetic (except oral arithmetic remaining to be given under standard I.), you will allow time enough to elapse for the completion of their exercises, say three quarters of an hour.

19. You will then call them name by name from the examina-

tion schedule to read, which you will hear each do, and, immediately afterwards, mark each in column ix. of the schedule for writing and arithmetic also, as far as time will permit. If this fails before you can go through the whole of them, you will mark the reading only of all, and the slate work of those who do not write on paper, and you will bring the rest of the papers away and mark them at home. You must be careful to collect and keep them *in the order of the names upon the schedule*, otherwise you will not easily be able to put the right marks against the right names. When you pass a paper, you should write P against the writing and arithmetic in it respectively, besides marking column ix. in the schedule.

20. Whether you mark the papers in the school, or reserve them, you should bring the whole away with you, and forward them to this office with your report. My Lords will probably appoint, from time to time, committees of inspectors and examiners to look over specimens and determine the means of fixing the minimum of each standard.

As a tentative standard, my Lords are of opinion that an exercise which in the ordinary scale of *excellent, good, fair, moderate, imperfect, failure*, would be marked *fair*, may pass. The word *fair* means that *reading* is intelligible, though not quite good; *dictation*, legible, and rightly spelt in all common words, though the writing may need improvement, and less common words may be misspelt; *arithmetic*, right in method, and at least one sum free from error.

21. My Lords are informed by Mr. Cook that from four to six hours will suffice for examining and marking 150 children. It may hereafter be needful, as the Royal Commissioners suggest, to employ additional agency, but experience must first be gained by a higher class of officers.

22. Under column vi. of the schedule children may be presented to you not belonging to the class (Article 4) for whose education the Parliamentary Grant is voted. Such children should be charged the full cost (about 30s. per annum) of their education at the least, and it is perfectly legitimate to charge

them more for the benefit of the rest of the school, if the managers have the opportunity of doing so. The presence of a limited number of such children among the rest has some obvious advantages besides those which are financial. It has also its danger; that, namely, of causing the poorer scholars to be neglected. Subject to the inspector's report, my Lords leave the managers of elementary schools to decide whether such children shall attend or not; they cannot bring grants to the school by their examination, and must not be included in the calculation of average attendance.

23. The children between six and seven will in all cases require a certain amount of oral examination, which may be performed for each of them at the same time as they read.
Report of the Committee of Council on Education (1862-3), xxi–xxiii

31 The revised syllabus
The Newcastle Commission thought that training colleges should concern themselves only with those subjects that a teacher was likely to require when he was teaching poor children. Accordingly the teacher training syllabus was drastically pruned to the bare essentials.

SYLLABUS FOR MALE CANDIDATES
*School Management**
1. To answer questions on the expedients of instruction in reading, spelling, writing, and other elementary subjects.
2. To draw up time tables for use in a school under given circumstances.

Grammar
1. The elements of grammar, including questions on Latin Accidence.

* Passages taken from the Reading Lesson-books, commonly used in schools, will be given in the papers on all subjects which admit of it, and candidates will be expected to show how they would explain such passages to children. Each paper will also contain questions on the *method of teaching* the elementary parts of the subject to which it relates.

I

2. To parse a passage from the 1st Book of Wordsworth's "Excursion" (December 1863).*

Composition

1. To convert a passage from the same Book (1863) into the order of prose, and to paraphrase parts of it.

2. To write plain prose upon a given subject.

Geography

1. To be able to describe† and draw‡ the map of the four quarters of the globe, and the map of each country in Europe (that of Great Britain in fuller detail).

2. To answer questions on the physical, political, and commercial geography of *one* quarter of the globe. In December 1863, *Africa*.

History

The outlines of the History of England.

The paper will contain questions in Scottish History previous to the union of the Crowns; and candidates in Scotland may confine themselves to those questions for the period which they embrace.

Euclid

The first two books, with simple deductions from the propositions.

Economy

Elementary questions in sanitary and other practical science of common application, and in political economy. The 4th Book in the Reading Series of the Christian Knowledge Society, or of the Irish Commissioners, or of any similarly graduated

---

* It should be carefully read through in short portions, *in illustration of the English Grammar used.*

† The term "describe" is confined to *words*, as distinguished from *drawing.*

‡ The neatness as well as the correctness of these outlines will be taken into consideration. The degree of longitude and latitude must be given, in order to obtain *full* credit for the exercise.

series of Reading Lessons for schools, contains matter on which these questions will be founded.

Vocal Music*

1. Notation in the treble and bass clefs, time, accent, and the major and minor scales.
2. To write down, in correct time, short and simple passages played in the presence of the candidate.

Drawing

[N.B.—This exercise does *not* form part of the *December* examination. Annual examinations, *in drawing only*, are held at each of the *training colleges* under inspection some time in November, and at the various *local drawing schools* in connexion with the Department of Science and Art at times to be learnt from the masters of those schools. The value of the exercises is marked, and the marks carried to each candidate's total for a certificate.]

Any *two* (but not more) of the following exercises, for which the candidate may not have been registered as successful by the Department of Science and Art since the 24th of February 1857:—

1. Drawing free hand from flat examples.
2. Linear Geometry by aid of instruments.
3. Linear Perspective.
4. Shaded drawing from objects.
5. Objects from memory.

* This *paper* is not given to any candidate who does not produce a certificate signed by the principal of the training school, that *"he has such an amount of musical skill, vocal or instrumental, as is sufficient for the purpose of teaching children to sing from notes."* Acting teachers who are candidates must produce a similar certificate from some competent person, such as the organist of their church, etc.

Report of the Committee of Council on Education (1862–3), xxxiv–xxxv

32 Matthew Arnold   Payment by results

Matthew Arnold, the most famous of the government inspectors, detested payment by results (also known as the
Revised Code).

I cannot say that the impression made upon me by the
English schools at this second return to them has been a hopeful
one. I find in them, in general, if I compare them with their
former selves, a deadness, a slackness, and a discouragement
which are not the signs and accompaniments of progress. If I
compare them with the schools of the continent I find in them
a lack of intelligent life much more striking now than it was
when I returned from the continent in 1859.

This change is certainly to be attributed to the school legislation of 1862. That legislation has reduced the rate of public
expenditure upon schools, has introduced the mode of aid which
is commonly called *payment by results*, and has withdrawn from
teachers all character of salaried public servants. These changes
gratify respectively one or other of several great forces of public
opinion which are potent in this country, and a legislation
which gratifies these ought perhaps to be pronounced successful. But in my report to the Royal Commission of 1859 I said,
after seeing the foreign schools, that our pupil-teachers were, in
my opinion, "the sinews of English public instruction;" and
such in my opinion they, with the ardent and animated body of
schoolmasters who taught and trained them, undoubtedly were.
These pupil-teachers and that body of schoolmasters were
called into existence by the school legislation of 1846; the
school legislation of 1862 struck the heaviest possible blow at
them; and the present slack and languid condition of our
elementary schools is the inevitable consequence.

The rate of pupil-teachers to scholars in our elementary
schools was, in 1861, one pupil-teacher for every 36 scholars; in
1866 it was only one pupil-teacher for every 54 scholars. At the
recent examination of candidates for admission at Stockwell,
where schoolmistresses for British schools are trained, there were

75 girls as candidates for 52 vacancies; but at the Borough Road Training College, on which these schools depend for their supply of schoolmasters, there were only 53 candidates for 72 vacancies. Throughout all the training colleges only 1,478 candidates presented themselves for admission last Christmas, whereas 2,513 candidates presented themselves in 1862. Yet the number of schools recruiting their teachers from this source had risen from 6,258 in 1861 to 8,303 in 1866, and the average population of such schools from 919,935 to 1,082,055.

The performance of the reduced number of candidates is weaker and more inaccurate than was the performance of the larger number six years ago, and for the last year or two has been becoming weaker and weaker. No inspector can be surprised at this who compares the present acquirements of the vast majority of the pupil-teachers of his district in the yearly examinations which they have to pass before him with those which he remembers 10 years ago. Nor, again, can this difference in their acquirements surprise him when he compares the slackness, indifference, and loose hold upon their profession which is to be remarked in the pupil-teachers now, and contrasts it with what he remembers 10 years ago. The service of the pupil-teacher was then given under an indenture which he was accustomed to regard as absolutely binding him for five years; now it is given under an agreement which expressly declares itself to be always terminable by notice or payment. He then had $7\frac{1}{2}$ hours of instruction every week from the principal teacher, out of school hours and when all the attention of the principal teacher could be given to him; now he has only 5 hours of instruction, and these may be given in the night school, when the principal teacher's attention is divided. The work of teaching in school is less interesting and more purely mechanical than it used to be . . .

. . . To pass from the teachers to the schools. I cannot, with the recollection of the continental schools, and of what the schools of my district formerly were, fresh in my mind, say that the operation of the Revised Code has been in my opinion good for the schools if not for the teachers. My colleague, Mr. Bow-stead, says in his last report that on his best schools the Revised Code has produced little or no effect; on the great majority of his schools, which were neither very good nor very bad, it has produced an unfavourable effect; on his worst schools it has produced a good effect. In the best schools in my district the decay and discouragement of the teaching staff has not been without some bad effect on the school. I agree, however, with Mr. Bowstead that the instruction in these schools is in great measure independent of Government action, and is maintained at a high standard by the demands of the parents, in general of a class quite removed from poverty and fairly intelligent. I agree with him that in the majority of schools, neither very good nor very bad, the instruction has sensibly deteriorated. I hesitate to agree with him that even in the worst it has improved. In these schools the children's irregular attendance and premature leaving are and were the great causes of the school's badness, and not the insufficient attention paid to the younger children by the teacher. Children brought back for examination after a two months' absence fail, and children who have attended very irregularly fail, whatever care the teacher may have bestowed on teaching them; and meanwhile the better instructed top class, composed of children who stayed long enough to profit by careful teaching, who received this teaching, and who became, when they left school, a little nucleus of instruction and intelli-gence in their locality, has for the most part disappeared. The truth is, what really needed to be dealt with, in 1862 as at present, was the irregular attendance and premature with-drawal of scholars, not the imperfect performance of their duties by the teachers; but it was far easier to change the course of school instruction and inspection, and to levy forfeitures for imperfect school results upon managers and teachers, than to make scholars come to school regularly and stay there a suffi-cient time. . . . *Report of the Committee of Council on Education* (1867–8), 290–1, 295–6

33 The Revised Code defended

Matthew Arnold's attacks on the Revised Code are well known, but the majority of the inspectorate was more favourably inclined. These are the views of Mr Du Port.

... I ought to be specially qualified for the criticism of the Revised Code, for I was connected for two years (the last two of the old Code's existence) with what was then considered a first-rate London school, and on the coming in of the Revised Code I left England and remained in India for four years, so that on taking up my present work I came upon the Revised Code in the full working order of its fourth year's existence.

In that time, as I can unhesitatingly aver, it had in most schools remedied what I had always realized as the special blot upon the old system.

The Old Code worked admirably so far as the cleverest and oldest boys in a school were concerned. I dare say that at this moment our New Code schools could not as a rule send up equally successful candidates for prizes in Euclid or in history. But under the Old Code the lower classes received a very small share of the head teacher's care, and the duller children in the first class went to the wall in favour of the more interesting work of carrying on the elder and cleverer ones in their more advanced subjects. Now the mass of our children stay so short a time at school that they become perhaps not all, or perhaps only for a very short time, members of the first class; if therefore they are not well taught and trained in the lower classes they will never be taught at all. Again, of those in the first class of a school the cleverer and more advanced ones are just those who are able to carry on their own education with least aid from their teacher; whilst the duller and more backward ones are those whose only chance depends upon a teacher's more than ordinary pains. If they leave school unimproved they will forget everything, whilst the cleverer and more advanced ones on leaving school will naturally follow up on an education in which they have learned to find much pleasure. Here was the weak point of the old system; here lies the strong point of the new. *Now*, we press as closely into the grounding work of the junior classes as we do into the more interesting instruction of the elders. *Now*, we do not understand by a good school a school that can turn out 5 or 6 per cent, very clever scholars; but we say of a school in which 5 or 6 per cent can win prizes in all manner of subjects, whilst 94 or 95 per cent are learning nothing well and are developing no intelligence, that the school is bad, and that it quite fails in its duty as an educator of the people.

In another point, very similar to this, I see daily the advantages of the New over the Old Code. In the oral lessons under the Old Code, whether in geography, history, or scripture, it was very generally the fashion to allow a whole class to call out its answers altogether; hardly ever were the children pressed to answer one by one, and the evils of that system hardly need to be pointed out, they are now so patent to those who have seen the individualizing work of the New Code. I have seen, under the Old Code, a first class take visitors by storm with their ready replies (all with one voice) to their teacher's oral questions; but what was this generally worth? As a rule, in a class of 30, there would be five or six sharp children who alone learned anything individually, and they would start the answer to the teacher's questions, whilst the rest of the class, catching the cue from them, would co-respond with them. Take out those five or six clever children and the class, even collectively, could answer nothing.

And the weakness of that exclusive use of the simultaneous system in oral teaching is, that as all are to reply in chorus all must use the same words; hence arises a stereotyped form of question and answer which may succeed in developing memory but which must fail to awaken intelligence. The individualizing system of the New Code is rapidly removing from our annual grant schools this most fatal defect in oral instruction.

It has been said, however, that the Revised Code by its demands for individual grounding in reading, writing, and sums has lost to us the intelligence-awakening influence of the Old Code's favourite subjects, geography, grammar, and history.

I consider that up to the coming out of the Minute of February 1867, in which extra money grants were connected with the successful teaching of such subjects as the above, the Revised Code quite rightly ignored them. The gross want of lower class accuracy that obtained under the Old Code was only just being worked off by the end of 1866; and indeed there are still many schools in which the lack of good grounding has not yet been removed, and for which the time for introducing extra and higher subjects has not yet therefore come.

First let a school be thoroughly in working order from top to bottom as regards accuracy of elementary grounding, then extra subjects, such as history, geography, or grammar, can be introduced; and that not only without creating any risk of the children's failing in our individual test of their successful grounding in elementary subjects; but, by stimulating their intelligence, these extra and higher subjects of instruction will make them infinitely more self-confident and easy under an inspector's examination. . . . *Report of the Committee of Council on Education* (1869–70), 66–8

34 The Revised Code readers

Payment by results made teachers critical of the dreary material and long words in reading books. They insisted on new books, better adapted to helping children through the examinations. In the 1860s school readers were revised and much improved. This extract, of a reader prepared for children in Catholic schools, is typical of the new style.

THE FRUITS OF DISOBEDIENCE

| when-ev-er | obe-dient | sud-den-ly |
| neigh-bour | shoul-der | en-e-my |

Simon Lee had a bad trick of throwing stones. His father had often told him not to do it; but Simon was not an obedient boy. It is true he left off throwing stones when his father was near him, for fear he should be punished; but whenever he thought that he was not seen, he amused himself in the same idle manner.

He did a great deal of mischief. Sometimes his stones hit other persons in the street; sometimes they hurt the horses that were passing, and made them restive; and sometimes they went over the neighbours' hedges, and broke down their finest flowers.

A gentleman lived near Simon's house who had a son named Arthur. Arthur was not much more obedient than Simon was. He did not throw stones, indeed; but when his parents told him not to do a thing, he often said to himself, "What harm can there be in it? I will only do it this once," and so on.

One day Arthur's father had been shooting the sparrows that were picking up the seeds in the garden. He had his gun with him, and it was loaded. Suddenly he was called into the house to see someone who wanted him; and as he went away he called out to Arthur, "Arthur, I shall be back presently; mind you do not touch the gun." He stayed away some time, and Arthur began to think he should like to play with the gun. "What harm will it do, so long as I do not fire it off?" he thought; "I will only shoulder it, and march about like a soldier." So he shouldered the gun, and then he thought he would present it, and pretend to be shooting an enemy. Just then Simon, who was on the other side of the hedge, threw a great stone, and it hit Arthur on the eye. The pain was so great that it made him drop the gun, which went off, and the shot entered Simon's leg. The cries of the two boys brought their fathers to the spot; they were carried home and taken care of. But they paid dearly for their disobedience. Simon was lamed for life, and Arthur lost the sight of one of his eyes. How often both must have wished that they had learned to do as they were bid!

Home or School Lesson

Learn spelling of words in column, and copy sentences:

| there | *There* is a wide difference between *their* opinion |
| their | and yours. |

threw   Frederick *threw* the stone *through* the window.
through

Burns's Standard Reading-Book adapted to the requirements of the revised code, No III (1867), 41–2

PART FIVE

The 1870 Act and Beyond

Two factors were responsible over the last part of the nineteenth century for the steadily increasing allocation of the national budget to education. The child population itself rose sharply, and industry, now facing increasing foreign competition, looked for a modicum of education in young people. The educational facilities required by the country were now quite beyond the resources of the voluntary societies. In the 1860s the campaign for state education gained momentum (35) and in 1870 a new education bill was introduced (36). The 1870 Education Act made it obligatory for local authorities to establish schools if the number for an area was deemed inadequate (37).

Over the final thirty years of the century educationists were less preoccupied by religion. The syllabus itself had already been secularised, and there was more emphasis on preparing the child to cope with problems such as poverty (38) and drunkenness (39). The provision of free meals (40) and higher education for working-class children (41) became political issues. Payment by results was eventually abolished (42) and the Committee of Council set itself to grappling with the questions of educational philosophy that are familiar to us today— the need for the teaching profession to look beyond the examination process, and the need for society to recognise that its schools must be more than education factories (43).

35 The National Education League
However hard the voluntary societies tried to keep pace with

the increasing child population, provision of sufficient school places was well beyond their resources. While the government deliberated on what form of support to give to education, various interest groups were working on their propaganda campaigns. The most articulate, best organised and influential group was the Birmingham-based National Education League, whose objects are set out in this handbill.

NATIONAL EDUCATION LEAGUE
CENTRAL OFFICE,
17, ANN STREET, BIRMINGHAM

GEORGE DIXON, M.P., Chairman of Council

JOSEPH CHAMBERLAIN, *Chairman of Executive Committee.*	J. THACKRAY BUNCE, *Chairman of Publishing Committee.*
JOHN JAFFRAY, J.P., *Treasurer.*	R. F. MARTINEAU, *Chairman of Branches Committee.*
JESSE COLLINGS, *Honorary Secretary.*	REV. C. CLARKE, F.L.S., *Chairman of Statistical Committee.*
WILLIAM HARRIS, *Chairman of Finance Committee.*	FRANCIS ADAMS, *Secretary.*

OBJECT.

The establishment of a system which shall secure the Education of every Child in the Country.

MEANS.

1.—Local Authorities shall be compelled by law to see that sufficient School Accommodation is provided for every Child in their district.

2.—The cost of founding and maintaining such Schools as may be required shall be provided out of Local Rates, supplemented by Government Grants.

3.—All Schools aided by Local Rates shall be under the

management of Local Authorities and subject to Government Inspection.

4.—All Schools aided by Local Rates shall be Unsectarian.

5.—To all Schools aided by Local Rates admission shall be free.

6.—School Accommodation being provided, the State or the Local Authorities shall have power to compel the attendance of children of suitable age not otherwise receiving education.

National Education League Handbill, c 1870

36 The Elementary Education Bill

W. E. Forster, vice-president of the Council on Education, introduces the new Education Bill of 1870.

ELEMENTARY EDUCATION BILL
LEAVE. FIRST READING.

MR. W. E. FORSTER, in rising to move for leave to bring in a Bill to provide for public Elementary Education in England and Wales, said: If ever an apology was due to the House it is due from me to-night;—for, in expounding the principles of a measure so important as that which I have the honour to bring forward, the House might very well expect that clearness and facility of expression, of the want of which I am painfully conscious, and I can assure them that if I allowed myself to dwell upon my own deficiencies I should be hardly able to address them. But I confess I forget these deficiencies, and I believe the House will also forget them, in the important work we all of us have to try this evening to begin.

The subject of primary education is, indeed, one of great and serious importance, and I believe we approach it with a due regard to its importance. We approach it not merely with the hope of doing great good, by removing that ignorance which we are all aware is pregnant with crime and misery, with misfortune to individuals and danger to the community, but with the knowledge that it is possible, in a measure of this kind, with an intention to do good, to do harm. The question of popular education affects not only the intellectual but the moral training of a vast proportion of the population, and therefore we must not forget that in trying to do great good it is possible to do harm. I am sure, therefore, we all feel that a grave responsibility rests on the House; and whilst there is a feeling of urgent necessity of dealing with the question, there is also a feeling that it must be dealt with wisely and with great care. The knowledge that that feeling of responsibility is acknowledged by the House relieves me of a double task.

I need not detain the House with any reasons for bringing an Education Bill forward, nor need I ask hon. Members opposite to divest themselves of all party considerations in regard to this measure. I will not ask them to do so, because I feel confident they will do so. There never, I believe, was any question presented by any Government to this House which more demanded to be considered apart from any party consideration; nor do I believe there ever was a House of Commons more disposed so to consider it than the House I am now addressing.

Before I enter into details, I will make one remark with regard to the spirit in which the Government has framed this measure. I rejoice that of late the country has manifested so much interest in the subject. A great many meetings have been held, and, as was naturally to be expected, those who take part in them have divided themselves, more or less, into two camps. Those engaged at present in educational efforts endeavour to take care that they should not be unduly interfered with, while, on the other hand, those who say there ought to be a great improvement advocate systems more or less new. I have seen it stated that the Government measure will be a compromise between these two principles; but I may at once say that the Government has not brought forward this measure with any notion of a compromise. It is a measure too important to be dealt with in such a manner. It is our duty to look at the question on all sides, and without professing that we, and much less

I, know more about this question than those gentlemen who have been doing their duty in pressing their particular views on the attention of the country, yet it is our duty to look around the question on both sides of it, and to consider the lessons of the past as well as the wants of the present.

Again, we are well aware that by no Bill dealing with this matter can we hope to effect real good, unless it be a Bill which does not merely meet present necessities, but also is capable of development, so as to meet the necessities of the future. Indeed, no Bill would really meet the needs of to-day unless its provisions are likewise adapted to meet the needs of to-morrow.

I am not going to detain the House with any long statement of facts, and still less do I intend to weary you with statistics; but there are two great categories of facts which I would beg you to bear in mind. The first is the broad fact of what we have existing at this moment in regard to primary education. I shall confine myself to that, respecting which we are pretty accurately informed, because it relates to the schools to which we vote Government money. Last year I moved the Education Estimate, and in addition to the money required for the central office, for Inspectors, and for normal schools, I asked for an annual grant of about £415,000 for primary schools in England and Wales. Of those schools about 11,000 were day schools and 2,000 night schools. The number of children upon the registers of those schools was about 1,450,000, and the average attendance about 1,000,000, representing, therefore, the education more or less imperfect of nearly 1,500,000 children. I say the education, according to these Returns, is very imperfect, because the attendance is very irregular, nevertheless the figures I have just referred to represent also a great amount of voluntary zeal, and much willingness on the part of parents to send their children to school. Now, while alluding to voluntary zeal, I must be allowed to state that I think no one could occupy my office without being fully aware of what the country owes to the managers of the schools at present in receipt of Government grants. Both before and during my tenure of that office I have had many opportunities of seeing those gentlemen at work, particularly ministers of religion of all denominations, though perhaps it has been my lot to see more of the clergy of the Church of England than of others. I have seen them at their work, and tried to help them occasionally; I know the sacrifices they have made, and not for a moment do I believe it possible that any-one who considers this question will disregard what they have already done, or will wish to do without their aid in the future. I sometimes hear it objected that they gain great influence by their efforts in promoting education. I believe they have not worked in order to attain that object, though far distant be the time when, in England, self-denying exertions, such as many of these gentlemen have made, will not give them influence!

Having alluded to what we already have, I will now ask— "What is it that we have not?" More or less imperfectly about 1,500,000 children are educated in the schools that we help— that is, they are simply on the registers. But, as I had the honour of stating last year, only two-fifths of the children of the working classes between the ages of six and ten years are on the registers of the Government schools, and only one-third of those between the ages of ten and twelve. Consequently, of those be-tween six and ten, we have helped about 700,000, more or less, but we have left unhelped 1,000,000; while of those between ten and twelve, we have helped 250,000, and left unhelped at least 500,000. Some hon. Members will think, I daresay, that I leave out of consideration the unaided schools. I do not, how-ever, leave them out of consideration; but it so happens—and we cannot blame them for it—that the schools which do not receive Government assistance, are, generally speaking, the worst schools, and those least fitted to give a good education to the children of the working classes. That is the effect of the pre-sent system. Exceptions, no doubt, may be picked out; but, speaking generally, my assertion is borne out by the Reports presented annually by our Department, and particularly by the Report of last Session. I may also refer to the Report which will be speedily in the hands of hon. Members, in consequence of the

K

Motion made last year by the hon. Member for Stoke (Mr. Melly), concerning the educational condition of four great towns—Liverpool, Manchester, Leeds, and Birmingham. That Report, I have reason to believe, will abundantly confirm my statement that we cannot depend upon the unaided and un-inspected schools. I have not myself had the opportunity of reading that Report, for I was so anxious that it should be laid before the House with the least possible delay that I did not keep it in my hands for a single hour. But I have had the privilege of corresponding with the two gentlemen who conducted the inquiries; and therefore I believe I can give pretty correctly the figures with regard, at all events, to Liverpool, and they are figures which may well alarm us. It is calculated that in Liverpool the number of children between five and thirteen who ought to receive an elementary education is 80,000; but, as far as we can ascertain, 20,000 of them attend no school whatever, while at least another 20,000 attend schools where they get an education not worth having. In Manchester—that is, in the borough of Manchester, not including Salford, there are about 65,000 children who might be at school, and of this number about 16,000 go to no school at all. I must, however, add that Manchester appears to be better than Liverpool in one respect, that there are fewer schools where the education is not worth having. As a Yorkshireman, I am sorry to say that, from what I hear, Leeds appears to be as bad as Liverpool; and so also, I fear, is Birmingham.

I am not going to deal with facts at any length to-night. My noble Friend my predecessor (Lord Robert Montagu) takes a sanguine view of the present state of education, and quotes a deficiency in attendance of only 300,000 children. I will not now dispute his figures, which, indeed, would make out a case for a Bill; but I am afraid it is a far too sanguine view of the case. It is not, however, necessary to detain the House with any dispute as to the amount of educational destitution, because hon. Members will see, when they read the Bill, that the practical action of it will be limited to the proved need.

I have stated to the House what now exists, and I have endeavoured to form an estimate of what does not exist in regard to the education of the people. Now, what are the results? They are what we might have expected; much imperfect education and much absolute ignorance; good schools become bad schools for children who attend them for only two or three days in the week, or for only a few weeks in the year; and though we have done well in assisting the benevolent gentlemen who have established schools, yet the result of the State leaving the initiative to volunteers, is, that where State help has been most wanted, State help has been least given, and that where it was desirable that State power should be most felt it was not felt at all. In helping those only who help themselves, or who can get others to help them, we have left unhelped those who most need help. Therefore, notwithstanding the large sums of money we have voted, we find a vast number of children badly taught, or utterly untaught, because there are too few schools and too many bad schools, and because there are large numbers of parents in this country who cannot, or will not, send their children to school. Hence comes a demand from all parts of the country for a complete system of national education, and I think it would be as well for us at once to consider the extent of that demand. I believe that the country demands from us that we should at least try to do two things, and that it shall be no fault of ours if we do not succeed in doing them—namely, cover the country with good schools, and get the parents to send their children to those schools. I am aware, indeed, that to hope to arrive at these two results may be thought Utopian; but our only hope of getting over the difficulties before us, is to keep a high ideal before our minds, and to realize to ourselves what it is we are expected to try to do.

The first problem, then, is, "How can we cover the country with good schools?" Now, in trying to solve that problem there are certain conditions which I think hon. Members on both sides of the House will acknowledge we must abide by. First of all, we must not forget the duty of the parents. Then we must not forget our duty to our constituencies, our duty to the taxpayers. Though our constituencies almost, I believe, to a man would spend money, and large sums of money, rather than not do the work, still we must remember that it is upon them that the burden will fall. And thirdly, we must take care not to destroy in building up—not to destroy the existing system in introducing a new one. In solving this problem there must be, consistently with the attainment of our object, the least possible expenditure of public money, the utmost endeavour not to injure existing and efficient schools, and the most careful absence of all encouragement to parents to neglect their children. I trust I have taken the House thus far with me. Our object is to complete the present voluntary system, to fill up gaps, sparing the public money where it can be done without, procuring as much as we can the assistance of the parents, and welcoming as much as we rightly can the co-operation and aid of those benevolent men who desire to assist their neighbours. . . . Hansard's *Parliamentary Debates*, Third series, Vol CXCIX, col 438–444 (17 February 1870)

37 The Elementary Education Act, 1870

The Act compelled local authorities to establish rate-aided elementary schools in areas where there were not enough voluntary schools.

LOCAL PROVISION FOR SCHOOLS

. . . 4. For the purposes of this Act the respective districts, boards, rates and funds, and authorities described in the first schedule to this Act shall be the school district, the school board, the local rate, and the rating authority.

Supply of Schools

5. There shall be provided for every school district a sufficient amount of accommodation in public elementary schools (as herein-after defined) available for all the children resident in such district for whose elementary education efficient and

suitable provision is not otherwise made, and where there is an insufficient amount of such accommodation, in this Act referred to as "public school accommodation," the deficiency shall be supplied in manner provided by this Act.

6. Where the Education Department, in the manner provided by this Act, are satisfied and have given public notice that there is an insufficient amount of public school accommodation for any school district, and the deficiency is not supplied as hereinafter required, a school board shall be formed for such district and shall supply such deficiency, and in case of default by the school board the Education Department shall cause the duty of such board to be performed in manner provided by this Act.

7. Every elementary school which is conducted in accordance with the following regulations shall be a public elementary school within the meaning of this Act; and every public elementary school shall be conducted in accordance with the following regulations (a copy of which regulations shall be conspicuously put up in every such school); namely,

(1.) It shall not be required, as a condition of any child being admitted into or continuing in the school, that he shall attend or abstain from attending any Sunday school, or any place of religious worship, or that he shall attend any religious observance or any instruction in religious subjects in the school or elsewhere, from which observance or instruction he may be withdrawn by his parent, or that he shall, if withdrawn by his parent, attend the school on any day exclusively set apart for religious observance by the religious body to which his parent belongs:

(2.) The time or times during which any religious observance is practised or instruction in religious subjects is given at any meeting of the school shall be either at the beginning or at the end or at the beginning and the end of such meeting, and shall be inserted in a time table to be approved by the Education Department, and to be kept permanently and conspicuously affixed in every schoolroom; and any scholar may be withdrawn by his parent from such observance or instruction without forfeiting any of the other benefits of the school:

(3.) The school shall be open at all times to the inspection of any of Her Majesty's inspectors, so, however, that it shall be no part of the duties of such inspector to inquire into any instruction in religious subjects given at such school, or to examine any scholar therein in religious knowledge or in any religious subject or book:

(4.) The school shall be conducted in accordance with the conditions required to be fulfilled by an elementary school in order to obtain an annual parliamentary grant.

Proceedings for Supply of Schools

8. For the purpose of determining with respect to every school district the amount of public school accommodation, if any, required for such district, the Education Department shall, immediately after the passing of this Act, cause such returns to be made as in this Act mentioned, and on receiving those returns, and after such inquiry, if any, as they think necessary, shall consider whether any and what public school accommodation is required for such district, and in so doing they shall take into consideration every school, whether public elementary or not, and whether actually situated in the school district or not, which in their opinion gives, or will when completed give, efficient elementary education to, and is, or will when completed be, suitable for the children of such district.

9. The Education Department shall publish a notice of their decision as to the public school accommodation for any school district, setting forth with respect to such district the description thereof, the number, size, and description of the schools (if any) available for such district, which the Education Department have taken into consideration as above mentioned, and the amount and description of the public school accommodation, if any, which appears to them to be required for the district, and any other particulars which the Education Department think expedient.

If any persons being either—

(1.) Ratepayers of the district, not less than ten, or if less than ten being rated to the poor rate upon a rateable value of not less than one third of the whole rateable value of the district, or,

(2.) The managers of any elementary school in the district, feel aggrieved by such decision, such persons may, within one month after the publication of the notice, apply in writing to the Education Department for and the Education Department shall direct the holding of a public inquiry in manner provided by this Act.

At any time after the expiration of such month, if no public inquiry is directed, or after the receipt of the report made after such inquiry, as the case may be, the Education Department may, if they think that the amount of public school accommodation for the district is insufficient, publish a final notice stating the same particulars as were contained in the former notice, with such modifications (if any) as they think fit to make, and directing that the public school accommodation therein mentioned as required be supplied.

10. If after the expiration of a time, not exceeding six months, to be limited by the final notice, the Education Department are satisfied that all the public school accommodation required by the final notice to be supplied has not been so supplied, nor is in course of being supplied with due despatch, the Education Department shall cause a school board to be formed for the district as provided in this Act, and shall send a requisition to the school board so formed requiring them to take proceedings forthwith for supplying the public school accommodation mentioned in the requisition, and the school board shall supply the same accordingly. . . . Elementary Education Act, 33 & 34 Victoria, c 75

38 W. L. Blackley Self-help

Expenditure on poor relief was rising over the latter part of the nineteenth century. Public concern inevitably found its way into the school readers of the period. W. L. Blackley, the pioneer of social insurance, is the author of the school reader in which this lesson appears.

WHAT SHALL WE LIVE ON WHEN WE GROW TOO OLD TO EARN WAGES?

1. YOUNG people do not often take the trouble to think what will become of them if they live to grow old. They are strong and healthy, and fancy they will always remain so. But they have only to look round and count the neighbours whom they look upon as old people to see that in old age all men become feeble, and nearly all are sufferers. A young man would think a farmer or any other employer very foolish, if, about to pay for a day's work, he should employ a very old man while he could get a young man for the same money. So plain is it that the old man is not so able as the young, and that his labour is not worth so much.

2. Let the old man be ever so willing to work, he cannot earn, in old age, as much money as in youth. He has less strength, for his power is wearing out; he has less time to earn in, for he is much oftener sick than he was; he has less chance of help from friends, for most of his old friends are dead and gone. He needs better food, for his heart is weak; he needs better clothing, for old people feel cold a great deal more than young ones; he needs more visits from the doctor, because he is so often ailing; and he needs more help from others, because he cannot help himself as he used.

3. But not one of all these things that he wants so much can he get if he is so poor. And so he grows more and more needy, and more and more miserable, till some day the relieving officer comes with a cart and takes him away from the village where he has had his home all his life, and where nearly all his acquaintances live; and brings him off to the town to a house full of strangers; and his neighbours say, 'Ah! poor old So-and-So is gone to the workhouse'; and then he is forgotten, perhaps for a year or two, till the relieving officer brings him back once more

on the cart, but this time nailed up in a poor, shabby coffin, and they put him in the churchyard, and say a prayer over his grave, and then indeed he is forgotten altogether. The few who followed or who saw his coffin pass their doorway, which perhaps he himself had crossed hundreds of times, say, 'Well, that's the last of poor old So-and-So. He was as fine a fellow once as anyone, and could do a good day's work and earn a good day's wages. And yet he has had to be buried by the parish!'

4. Now, that is just what becomes of many thousands of people every year in our country, who were young people once, like those who read this book, and did not care to ask themselves the question, 'What will become of us if we live to grow old?' I hope that even these pages may help to show young people, in good time, that if they will only act in a common-sense way, they may feel quite secure against being buried by the parish, being without food in their hunger, without warmth in their winter, without help in their sickness, or without home in their age.

5. But if I show them this so plainly that they shall feel it must be true, they must not forget that if, in spite of such showing, they come at last to be poor and miserable and wretched in their old age, instead of being comfortable and well-cared for and happy, it will be their own fault; and that they will have self-reproach and real shame and disgrace added to their misery and sufferings.

6. For the poor, old, worn-out men and women whom the parishes bury every day now, may never have known how to keep themselves from beggary. But everyone who in youth has read this book through will have had the way put plainly before him, and will only have himself to thank at the end if, in spite of better knowledge, he spend his latter days in wretchedness instead of comfort. W. L. Blackley. *The Social Economy Reading Book* (1880)

L

30 Drunkenness

Drunkenness was one of the great social evils. This extract is taken from a 'temperance' school-reader.

FATTY DEGENERATION

1. WE have seen that *less oxygen absorbed* by the blood, means *less carbonaceous material oxidised* in the tissues and blood, and less heat produced.

But what becomes of the waste tissues and the sugar and fat which should be burnt up, and so destroyed, but *are not*?

2. The blood, being unable to rid itself of them in the natural way, stores them up as fat, in the tissues, under the skin, and in various parts, and the body is turned into a *storehouse for rubbish*! This accumulation of fat in an organ is termed *fatty degeneration*, which signifies that the organ is weaker and poorer, and less able to carry on its own work, through being loaded with fat, as, for instance, in the case of fatty degeneration of the *muscles*. These lose their elasticity and strength in proportion as they become packed with fat-cells.

3. The stout appearance, extra weight, and seeming robustness, which often follow indulgence in beer, stout, wines, etc., particularly those containing much sugar, are commonly regarded as proofs that the drink is very nourishing stuff. In reality they are unnatural, unhealthy, and a *source* of weakness and disease, and render the system less capable of *resisting* disease, and of *recovering* from sickness and accidental injuries, such as broken limbs, cuts, etc.

4. This is clearly shown by the experience of doctors and surgeons in our hospitals and infirmaries, where cases may be easily compared. How often can *no hope* of recovery be given, owing to the weak unhealthy condition of a patient's body, through the habitual use of strong drink! On the other hand, restoration to health and strength is often attributed by the doctor solely or mainly to the *abstinence* of the patient!

5. Stoutness, then, is not a measure of strength or health, but often the reverse, and a hindrance to activity. Men in training

for athletics, or any trials of bodily strength, are therefore careful to take *flesh-forming*, but *not fat-making*, food, and, for the time at least, to abstain entirely from the use of alcoholic liquors.

6. There is also fatty degeneration of the heart, of the liver, and other organs.

7. "In the beginning of this change (fatty degeneration) it is usual that the fatty substance is laid up outside and around the vital organs, or beneath the skin, where it is stored away in great abundance. In later stages, and occasionally from the first, the fatty particles are deposited within the minute structures of organs—in the muscular structure of the heart, or in the substance of the brain or kidney. The fatty degeneration, in this manner induced, is, of necessity, a permanent cause of feebleness, of premature decay, and, not unfrequently, of sudden death."—*"Health and Life," Sir B. W. Richardson.*

8. A drunkard's heart has been found to be almost buried in a great mass of fat, which had been placed there as upon a *rubbish heap*.

It will now be understood that the practice of mixing spirits with the food of cattle, in order to cause rapid fattening, is altogether contrary to nature. John Topham. *The Temperance Science Reading Book* (1893), 153–5

---

40 J. G. Fitch Free meals

One of the allegations made against the payment by results system was that it led to over-pressure of work for the school child. An eminent physician, Dr J. Chrichton-Browne, alleged in a paper that excessive school work was causing headaches and insomnia, serious diseases and even deaths among the school population. Some of his allegations may well have been questionable, but many pupils were in poor health because they were undernourished. Chrichton-Browne advocated free milk and school meals for poor children.

A senior school inspector, J. G. Fitch, was chosen by the

Committee of Council to refute such arguments. In the extract from his reply that is reproduced, he argues that a child's state of health was the concern of the parent, not the government.

. . . On the practical remedies suggested, I have only to remark that some of them seem to imply a radical misconception of the very limited and special function of a public elementary school. It is the office of such a school to provide healthy and suitable buildings, and to place the scholar in the midst of proper moral and mental surroundings, to furnish such rudiments of instruction as have been universally accepted as part of the necessary equipment for life; and in addition, to impart some knowledge of the world in which the scholar lives, the words he is to use, and the duties he has to discharge. And by means of well-varied discipline, by lessons on the facts of nature, and by a proper interchange of intellectual employments with physical or manual exercise, it seeks to give to the scholar pleasant associations with the business of learning, and to awaken in him a love of reading, of observation, and of self-improvement. All recent changes in the regulations of the Education Department, and in the practice of inspectors, have tended in this direction, and have been designed to make schools fulfil this purpose better. And a school which fulfils this purpose confers a distinct and permanent benefit on the community. But it cannot control *all* the conditions which affect a child's life. It cannot protect him from all the evils arising from poverty, sickness, or neglect at home. Dr. Browne says, truly, that "the sluggish intellects would brighten up and strengthen in grasp, could each of the weak children have two pints of new milk daily;" and he afterwards adds:—

"The children want blood, and we offer them a little brain-polish; they ask for bread and receive a problem; for milk, and the tonic-sol-fa system is introduced to them."

The answer to this is that a school is established for the purposes of instruction, and not for the purpose of dispensing new milk. And I trust the statesmen and philanthropists who are now considering this difficult and anxious question will think twice before complicating the problem of national education by mixing up with it the administration of food and medicine to the children of the poor. It is already a drawback to the success of the Education Act that it has unfortunately done a little to diminish the sense of parental responsibility. To enforce, in regard to any human duty, a legal obligation, is to weaken in some degree the sense of moral obligation. In regard to public education this is perhaps inevitable; for the amount of instruction which the State regards as a necessary qualification for citizenship is too costly a thing to be provided by a labouring man, and must therefore be furnished to his children by other aid. But the responsibility of caring for the food and health of young children belongs properly to the parent, and any public measures which relieved him of this responsibility might do far more mischief than is evident at first sight. Already I have had occasion to see how much harm is done by the benevolent efforts of persons who provide free dinners for children in the elementary schools; how many idle and improvident parents have been tempted to neglect their children, and to send them to school miserable and ill-clad, in the hope that sympathy might be awakened, and the children fed at other people's expense. Managers and clergy often tell me of the demoralising effect produced on many parents, who, not being paupers, are yet willing to claim free dinners for their little ones, and so to have more to spend in intemperance; and of the deep sense of wrong which is often felt by the self-respecting poor, who struggle to do their own duty to their families, and who see the children of fellow-workmen earning the same wages as themselves selected as the recipients of public charity. I am sure that if once it becomes understood that the State, or any public authority, is willing to provide nourishment and medical attendance for all the children in the public schools who seem to rebuire it, the influence on a large number of parents in diminishing their sense of responsibility may become a serious

public danger. . . . *Parliamentary Papers* 76–7, 1884, Vol LXI
(293)

___

41 Higher elementary schools
Higher elementary schools were established in the 1880s and
they competed with the grammar schools. The Cross Commission was not too happy about this development.

___

. . . However desirable these higher elementary schools may
be, the principle involved in their addition to our educational
system should, if approved, be avowedly adopted. Their in-
direct inclusion is injurious to both primary and secondary
instruction. If, therefore, the curriculum of higher elementary
schools is restricted within due limits, avoiding all attempts to
invade the ground properly belonging to secondary education,
and if due precautions are taken to secure that promising
children of poor parents are not excluded from the privileges to
be enjoyed in them, then we are of opinion that such schools
may prove to be a useful addition to our school machinery for
primary education. In certain cases the object of such schools
might be secured by attaching to an ordinary elementary
school a class or section in which higher instruction was provided
for scholars who had passed the Seventh Standard. In Scotland
liberal grants are now made to the managers of elementary
schools for advanced instruction to scholars who have passed
the highest standard, and we see no reason why English children
should not be afforded like assistance for continuing their education. This arrangement would facilitate the provision of such
higher instruction in the smaller and less populous school districts, and, for reasons already suggested, might be preferred, by
the authorities of some even of the larger districts, to the establishment of separate schools. We cannot therefore regard as
completely satisfactory the present position of the class of
schools to which we have referred. On the one hand they are
obliged to adapt their curriculum in such a way as to bring
them within the requirements of the Education Acts and of the

Code in order that they may obtain Government grants; whilst, on the other hand, their object is to provide a much higher education than is ordinarily understood by the word "elementary." There is beside a tendency to provide schools for children whose parents are in a position to pay fees sufficiently high to cover the expense of their education, and so to benefit persons in comfortable circumstances at the cost of the ratepayers and taxpayers; thus relieving parents of their proper responsibility for the education of their own children. Under these circumstances we think it is desirable that the State should recognise the distinction between elementary and secondary education to an extent not yet attempted. It is to be regretted that no practicable suggestion was made for extending any such higher education to rural districts, or, indeed, to places with populations below 10,000 or 15,000. A knowledge, for instance, of the principles of agriculture, which might be taught in a higher elementary school, if such existed in country places, might be of very great value to those children, who were hereafter to be engaged in agricultural labour. *Royal Commission on Elementary Education, Final Report*, 169, PP, 1888 [C. 5485], XXXV

42 The decline of payment by results

The Cross Committee was also unhappy about the payment by results system. In this part of their *Report* they suggest new ways of allocating the money that was available for education.

... In reference to the Parliamentary grant, and to payment by results, we are of opinion that the best security for efficient teaching is the organization of our school system under local representative authorities over sufficiently extensive areas, with full power of management and responsibility for maintenance, with well graduated curricula, a liberal staff of well-trained teachers, and buildings, sanitary, suitable, and well equipped with school requisites. That it should be the duty of the State to secure that all these conditions are fulfilled, and to aid local effort to a considerable extent, but leaving a substantial proportion of the cost of school management to be met from local resources other than fees of scholars, and by its inspection to secure that the local authority is doing its duty satisfactorily.

Such a system, in our opinion, would enable us to dispense with the present system of State grants variable according to the results of yearly examination and inspection, which, in our judgment, is far from being a satisfactory method of securing efficiency, and is forced upon the country by the irresponsible and isolated character of the management of the majority of our schools. In the meantime, as the system we prefer cannot in deference to existing denominational interests be secured, we recommend that there be a material change in the method of distributing the grant, that a larger fixed grant be given in consideration of increased requirements in the matter of staff premises and curriculum; that more money be given towards specific educational objects, such as the salaries of special teachers of science, drawing, cookery, etc., of local inspectors and organising masters, of the better instruction of pupil-teachers, and further aid to secure the diminution of their hours of work, especially during the earlier years of apprenticeship. Further aid should be given to small rural schools which especially need such aid and must be costly, and the grants should be larger to managers whose fees are low than to those who have a large fee income. As to the residue of the capitation grant, which we think must, under the present conditions of English education, continue variable, we recommend that the present system of paying a per-centage grant for the standard subjects shall cease; that there shall no longer be a general merit grant, but that the variable portion shall be distributed among the various subjects of instruction included in the recognised curricula, on the principle of the present class grant. We think, further, that schools which properly take up a fuller and more thorough course of studies should receive larger grants to meet their larger local expenditure. *Royal Commission on Elementary Education, Final Report* 249, PP, 1888 [C 5485], XXXV

___

43 Into the new century

Towards the end of the nineteenth century the Committee of Council was in the forefront of those who condemned 'utilitarian' education. The views expressed here might be considered as relevant for the 1970s as they were for the nineteenth century.

___

... The most important of all changes in connection with the internal working of our schools have been those resulting from the alteration in the system of inspection to which we referred in our last year's report. We then remarked that, though these alterations were still too recent to allow a final judgment to be passed upon their results, we regarded the changes which we had made in the rules of inspection as being of the utmost importance from the point of view of the efficiency of the schools. The reports which we receive from the inspectors as to the working of the new system of inspection are encouraging and satisfactory. It was our aim to relieve efficient schools and teachers from the false standard of educational excellence which the old system of examination tended to set up. We believe that a teacher who is competent for his duties and zealous in their discharge does his work best when he is given freedom in the choice of methods and liberty to adapt his course of instruction to the needs and abilities of his pupils. The most permanent and valuable results of education are not those which can be elaborately displayed on an annual field day. It is misleading to attempt to measure a teacher's educational skill or the more lasting effects of his instruction on the faculties and character of his pupils by a test which tends to throw the chief stress on the reproduction of a certain amount of knowledge on an appointed day. Such a system inevitably encourages sham rather than true education. It sets a premium on kinds of special preparation which are generally incompatible with the necessarily slow and less showy processes of thorough intellectual discipline. Children can usually be made to acquire, for a temporary purpose, a great deal of information which is afterwards quickly forgotten, and leaves behind it little permanent impress or lasting good. We are far from wishing to underrate the discipline involved, alike for teachers and pupils, in having to accomplish a given task by a given date. The duty of preparing for an appointed examination is within certain limits salutary in its influence on the work of all concerned. A definite aim stimulates them to orderly and systematic effort, and forms the habit of punctual preparation for an appointed test. But a system which makes this the chief aim of school-work is hurtful to the true efficiency of educational effort. It assesses its merits by a false standard. It induces superficial and fleeting excellence. It fixes attention on some of the less important results of the educational process, and too little on the educational process itself. The character-forming influences of a good school are so manifold that undue concentration of effort on one outcome of efficient instruction tends not only to throw into the shade much that is most valuable in itself, but indirectly to deter the teachers from giving the due measure of attention to other essential parts of their work. A school is a living thing, and should be judged as a living thing, not merely as a factory producing a certain modicum of examinable knowledge. . . . *Report of the Committee of Council on Education* (1897–8), XV–XVI

Suggestions for Further Reading

The history of education is best studied in a wider context. H. Perkin. *The Origins of Modern English Society 1780–1880* (1969) and R. K. Webb. *Modern England from the Eighteenth Century to the Present* (1969) are excellent background studies. Essential reading of a more specialised nature is R. D. Altick. *The English Common Reader, a Social History of the Mass Reading Public* (1963) and R. K. Webb. *The British Working Class Reader, 1790–1848* (1955). Two good general surveys of the history of education are W. H. G. Armytage. *Four Hundred Years of English Education* (1964) and S. J. Curtis. *A History of Education in Great Britain* (1967). The latter has a good bibliography. Brian Simon's *Education and the Labour Movement, 1870–1920* (1965) and *Studies in the History of Education, 1780–1870* (1960) are controversial and stimulating.

Of the many studies of elementary education the three most useful are M. Sturt. *The Education of the People* (1967), C. Birchenough. *History of Elementary Education in England and Wales from 1800 to the Present Day* (1938), and F. Smith. *A History of English Elementary Education* (1931). All have good bibliographies. A well documented study of Irish education is D. H. Akenson. *Irish Education, a History of Educational Institutions* (1970). For those interested in primary sources and research C. W. J. Higson. *Sources for the History of Education* (1967) and the typescript bibliographies published by the University of Leicester School of Education are indispensable.

163

Index